Tony Malone.

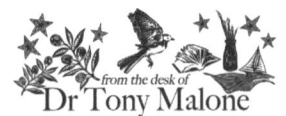

ISBN: 9798731526418

Published by:
Pied Wagtail Publishing

Printed using an environmentally considered process within the UK.

This edition: July 2022
First Printed in April 2021

Tony Malone is an artist and Human Rights Activist. He has spent over 20 years assisting rights causes across the world and continues to do so. You can find out more on their website: tonymalone.co.uk

HANAMI

Artwork by Tony Malone

Guest poem by Julie Newman

FLOWERS

I looked out of the window in the bright spring light
And the garden had changed, transformed overnight.
Where once the shrubs huddled against the day
The leaves shone bright, and the colours were gay
In the promise of much to come.

Looking again as I gazed at the beds of dark earth
The heads of green buds peeped through with the birth
Of young plants heralding spring. The lengthening days
Bring light to break the winter gloom, the warming rays
Gives a glimpse of the summer sun.

Looking again the flowers showed with bright brave faces,
Flashes of colour where once there were spaces.
Say farewell to the long winter nights too cold to dance
In the light of the moon, now we can rejoice, prance
And welcome the songs of spring.

Julie Newman, March 2021

THE ARTWORKS

Selected botanical artworks by Tony Malone.

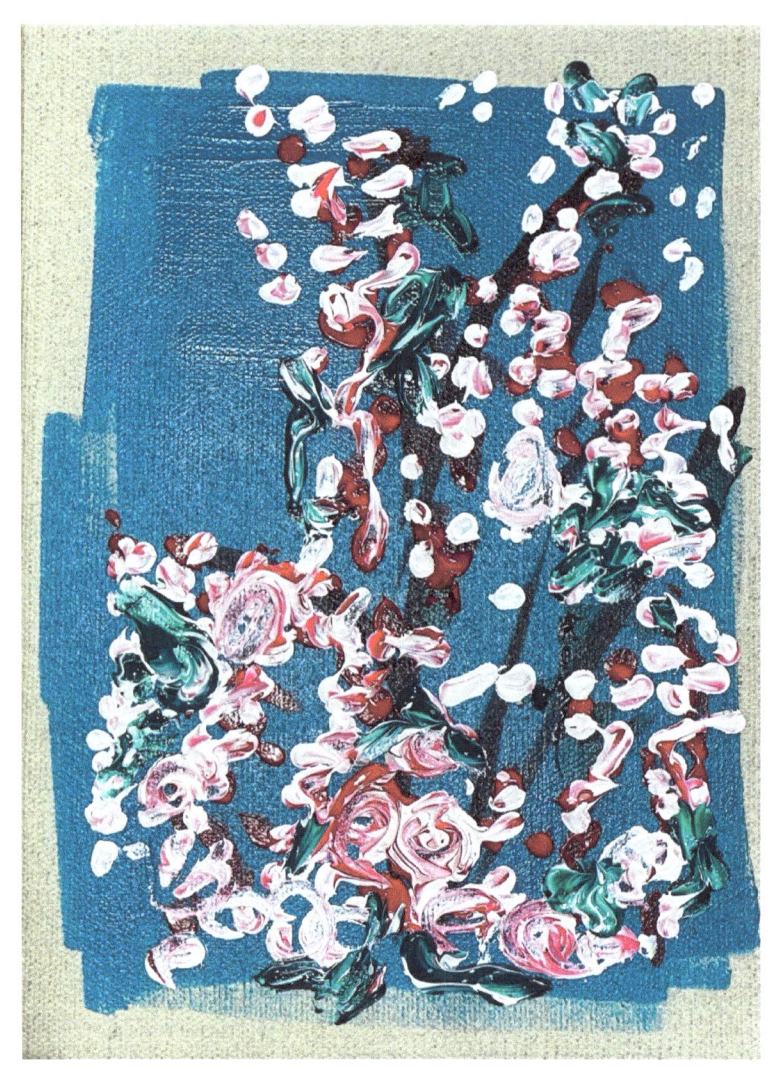

Rosebuds

Acrylic on canvas, 7x8"

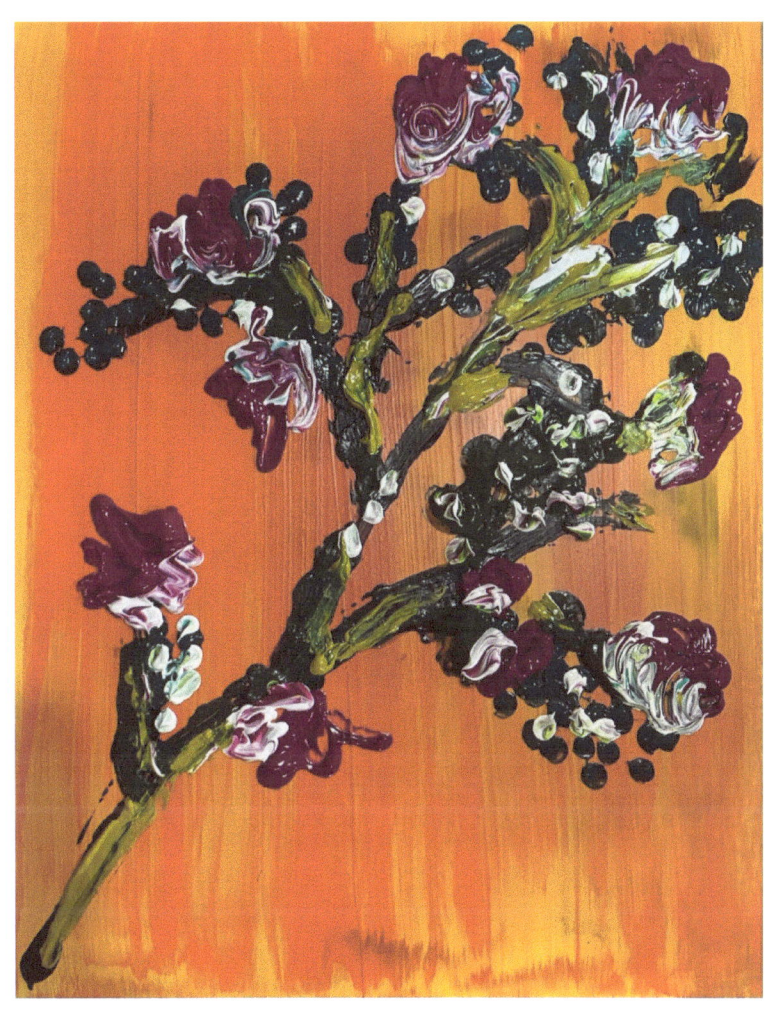

Thistle buds
Acrylic on board, 200x240mm

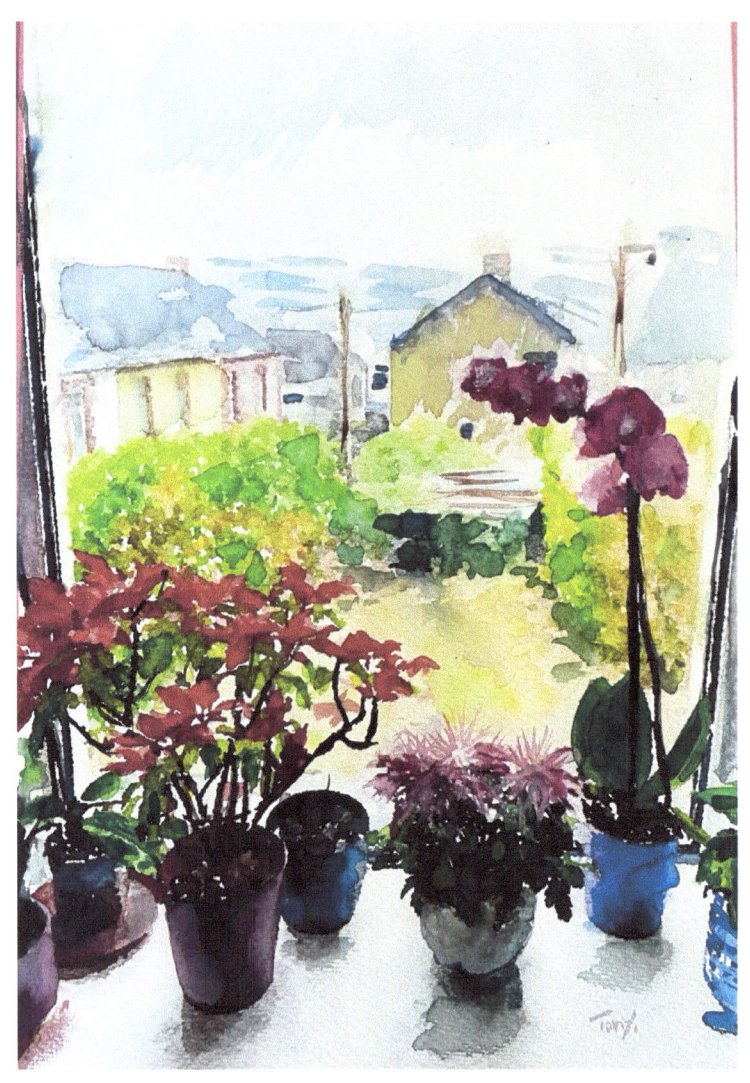

Houseplants

Watercolour on paper, 300x400mm

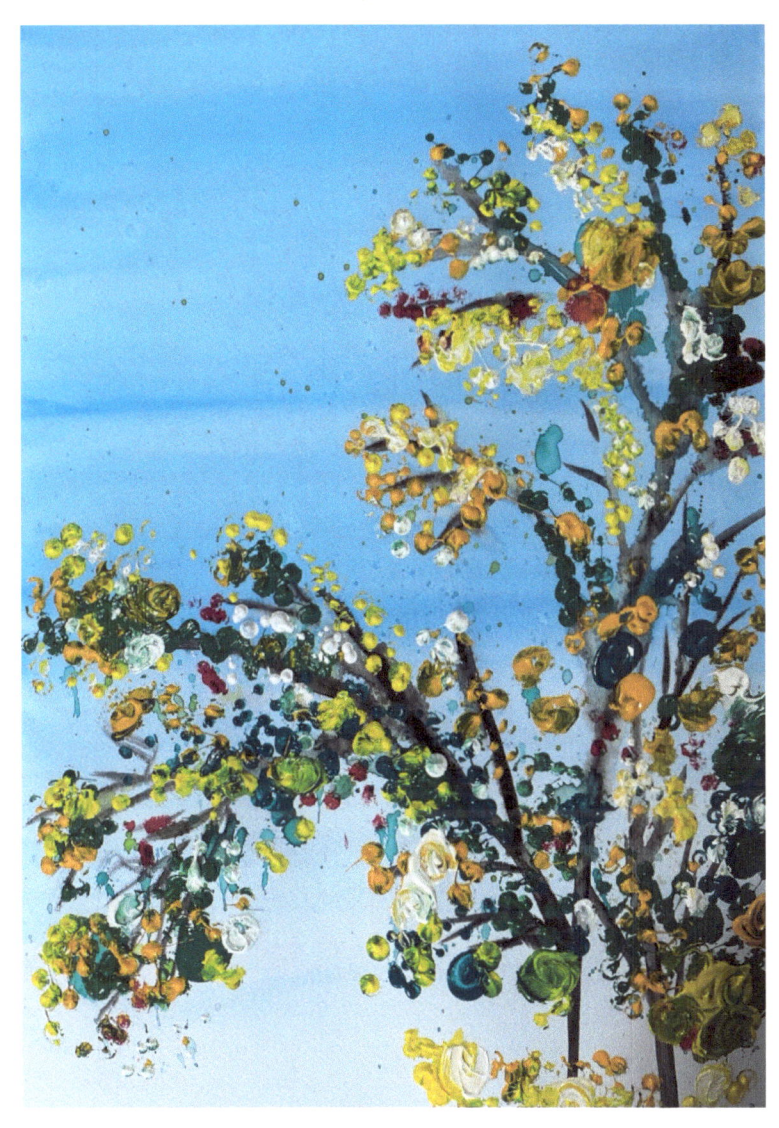

Gorse flower
Watercolour & Guaché on paper, 400x600mm

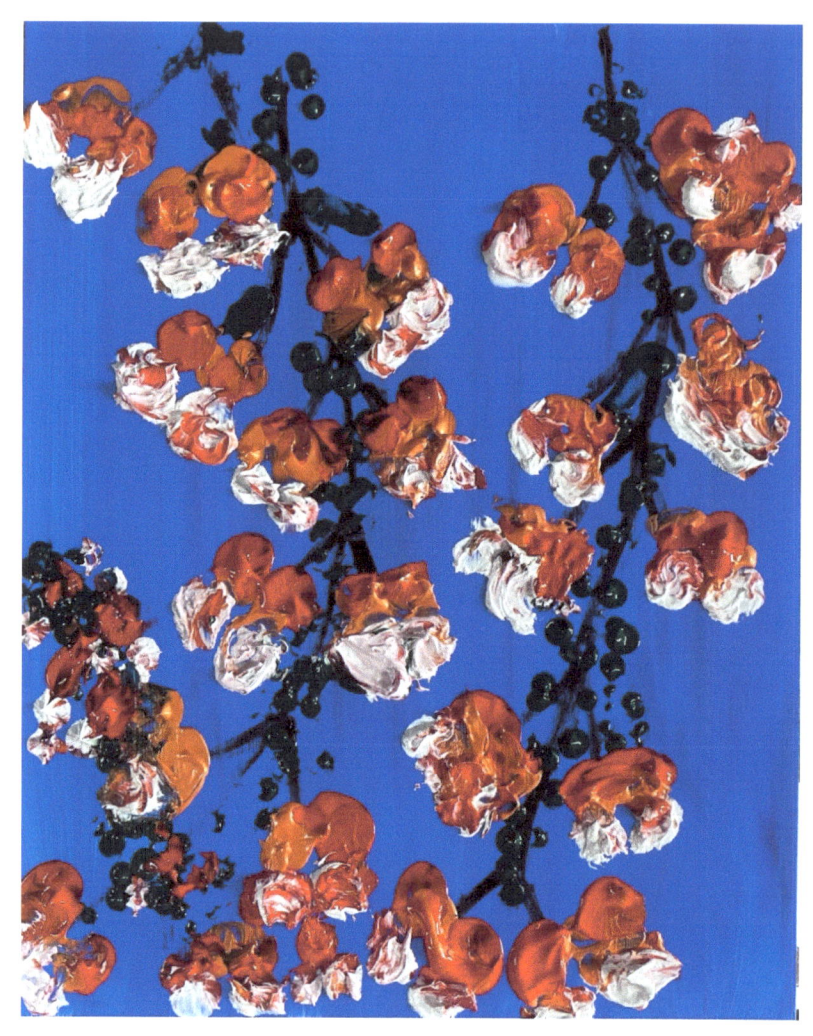

Blossom cascade
Acrylic on board, 200x240mm

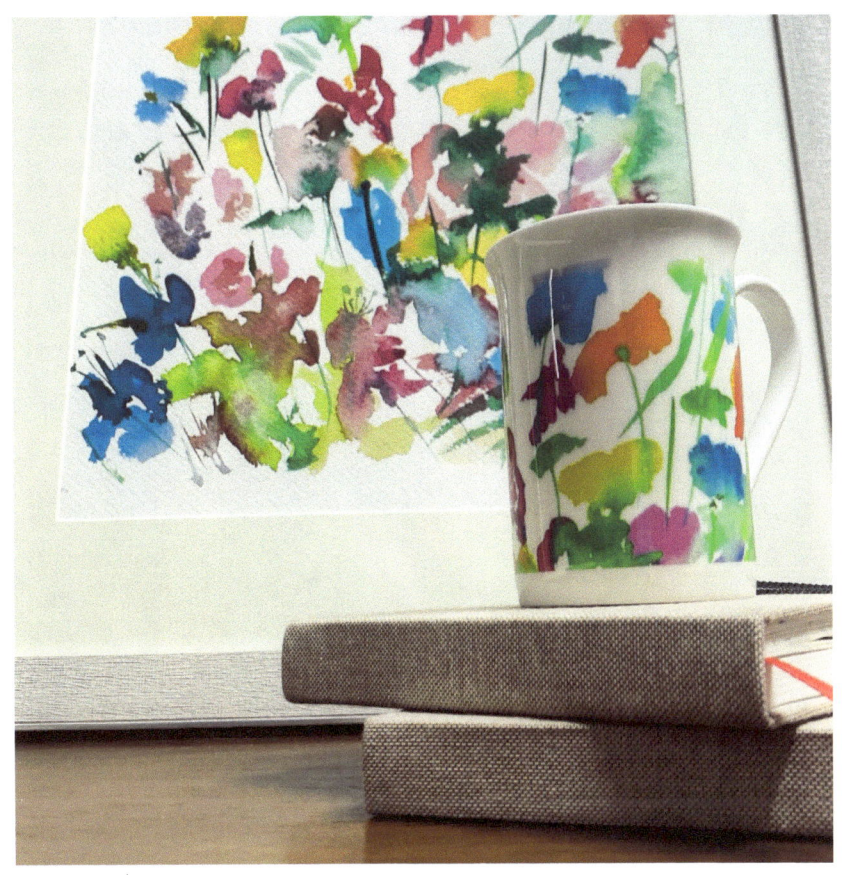

Wild spring flowers
Heat Inks on china-ware design

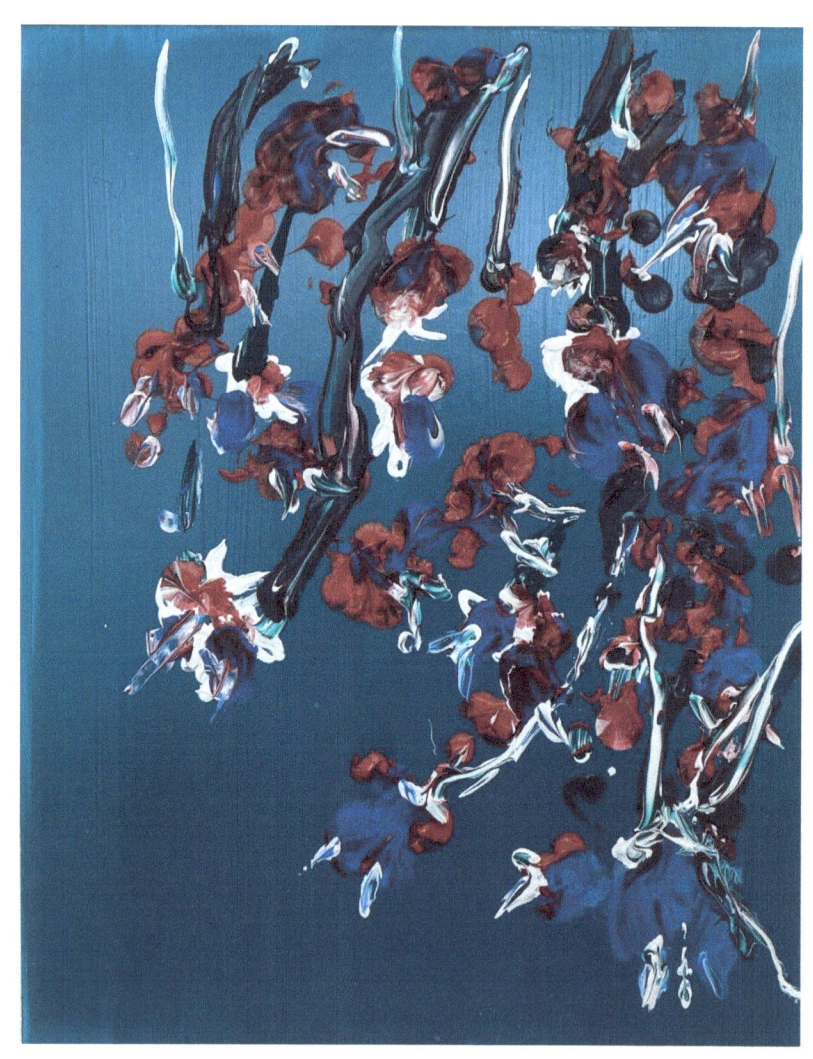

Falling fuscias
Acrylic on board, 200x240mm

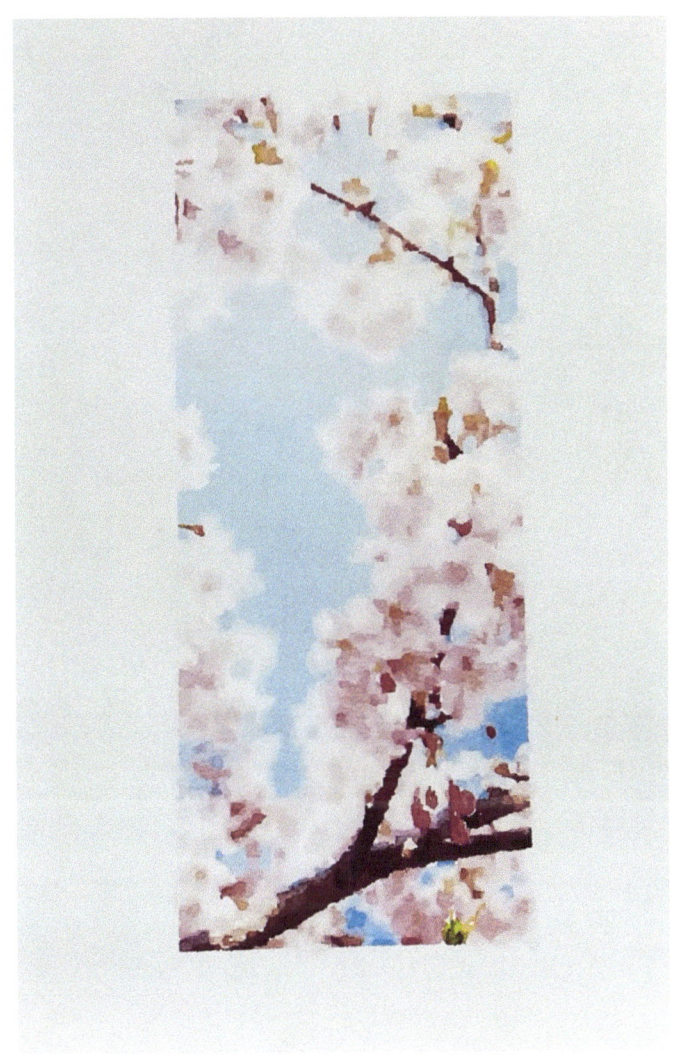

Cherry Blossom
Watercolour on paper, 300x400mm

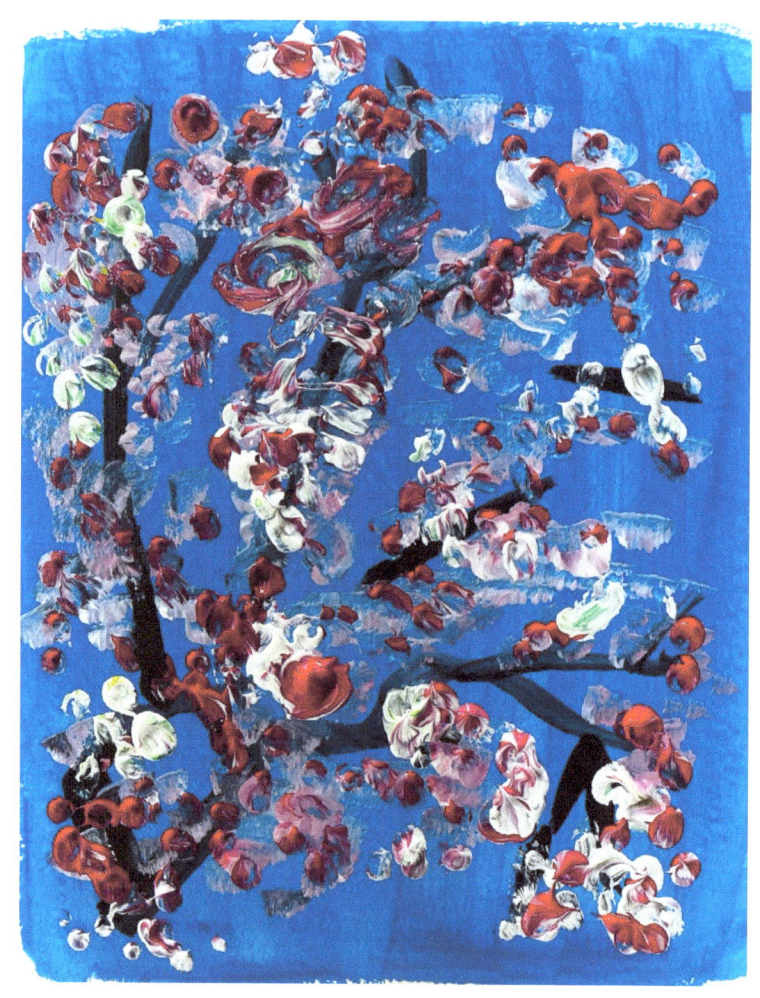

Hanami experiment 1
Watercolour on rough rag paper, 200x240mm

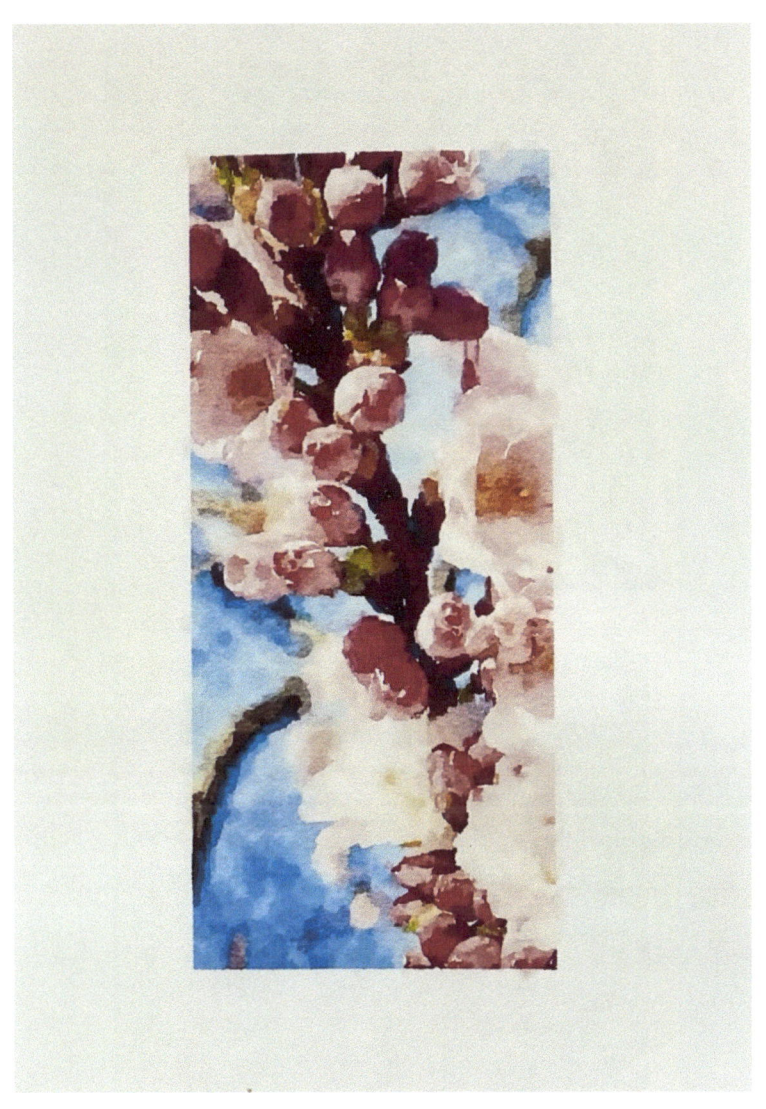

Cherry Blossom 2
Watercolour on paper, 300x400mm

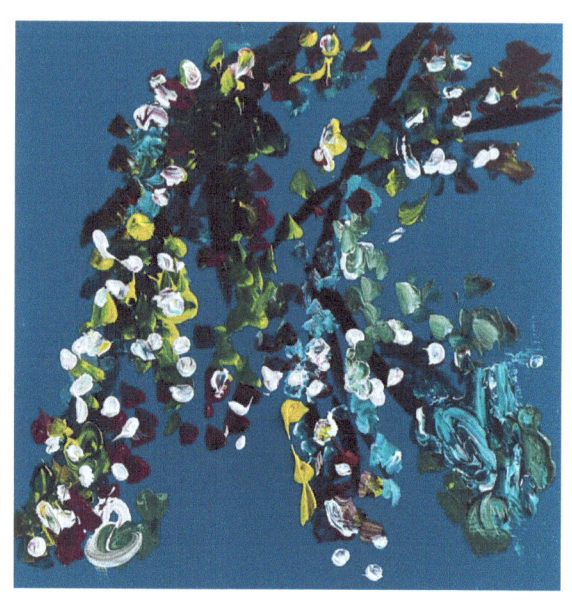

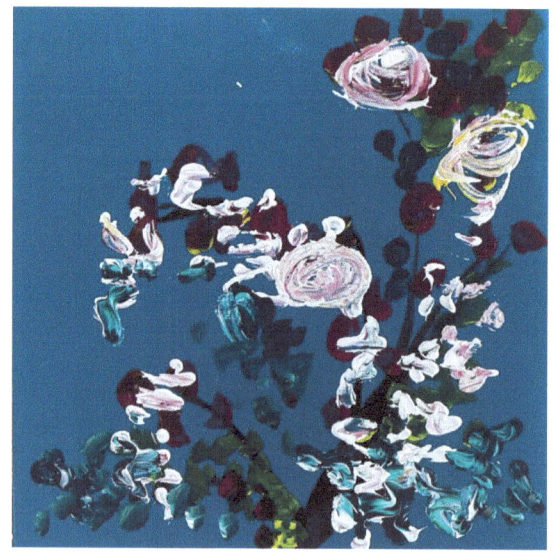

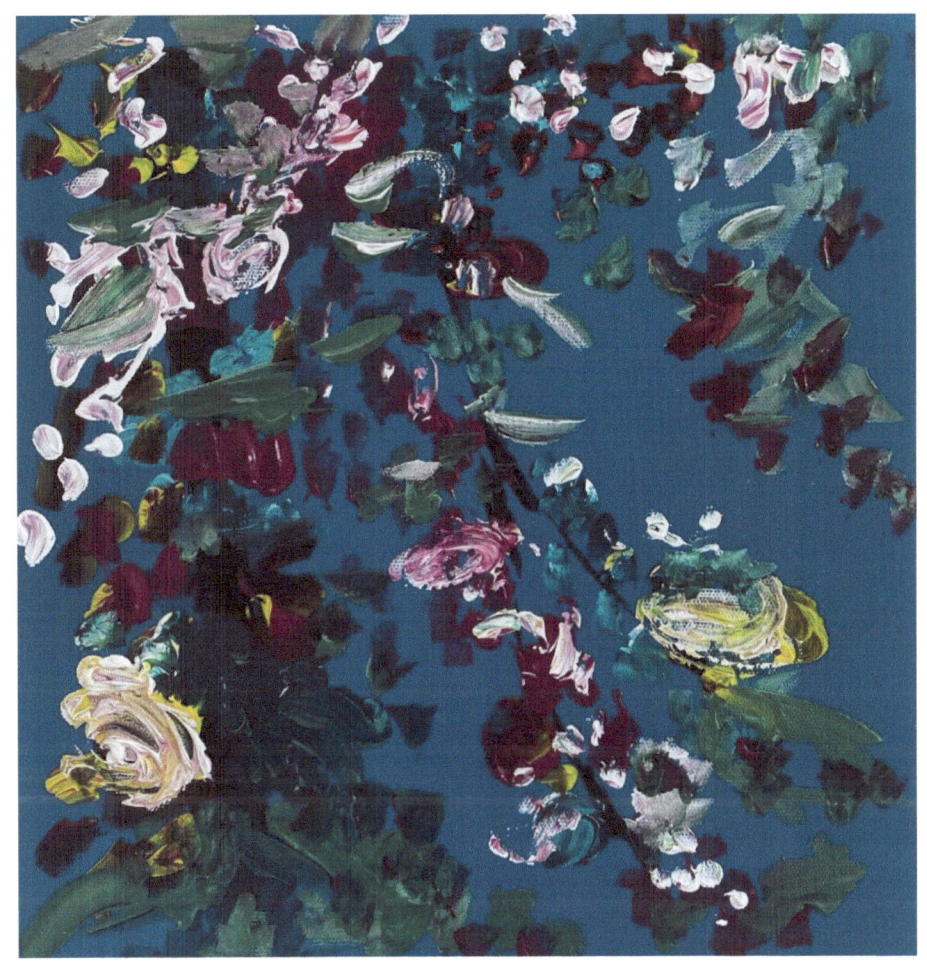

Dog rose blossom 3 Panels
Acrylic on canvas, 200x200mm

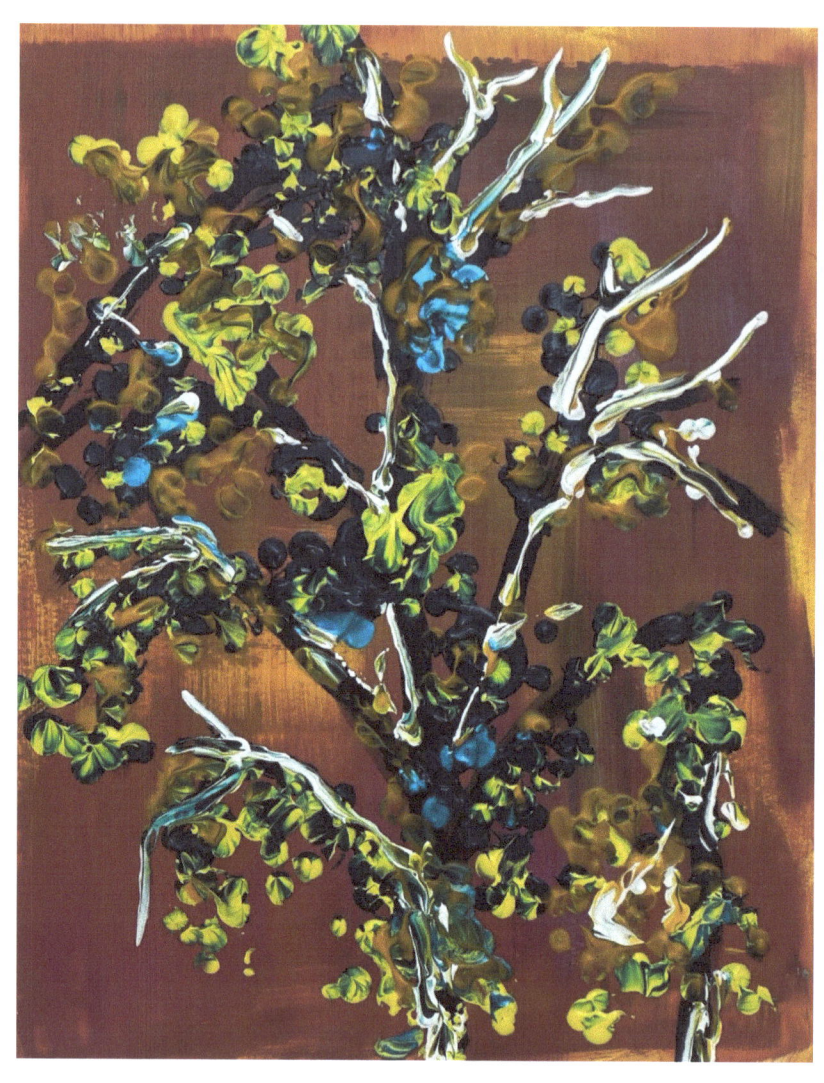

Spring growth
Acrylic on board, 200x240mm

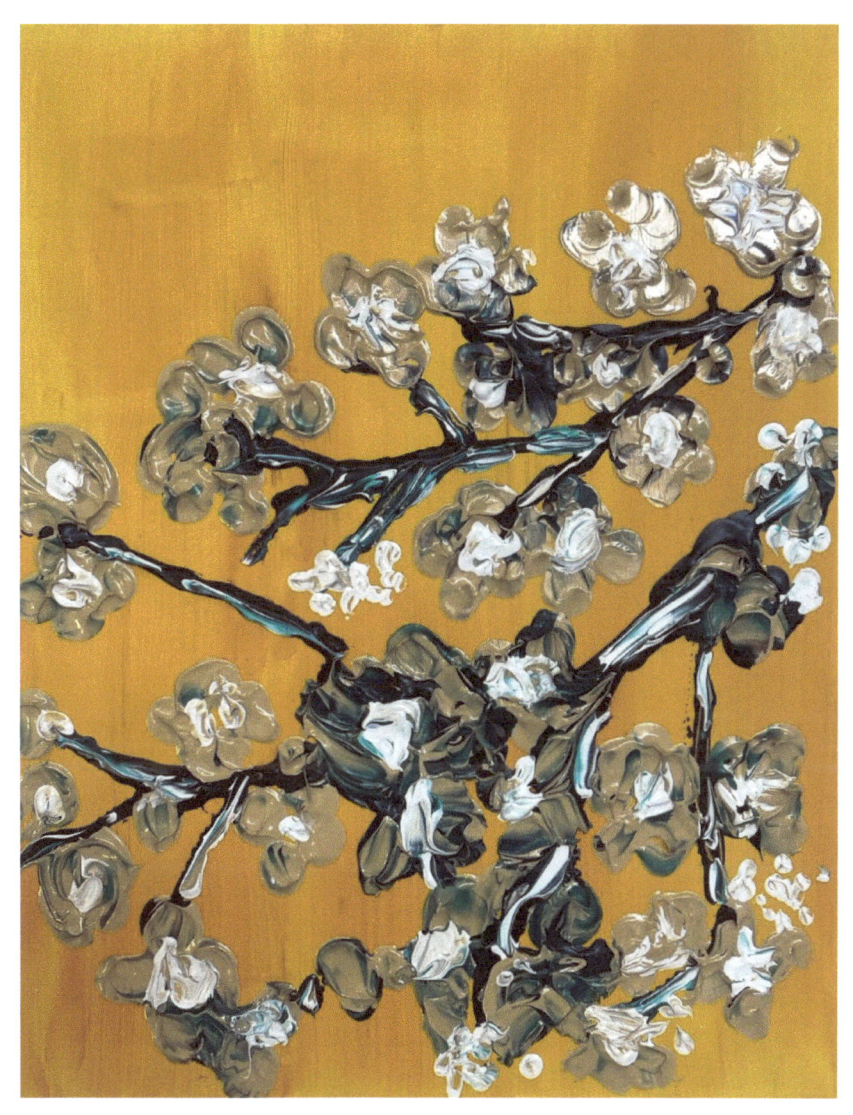

Almond blossom 1
Acrylic on board, 200x240mm

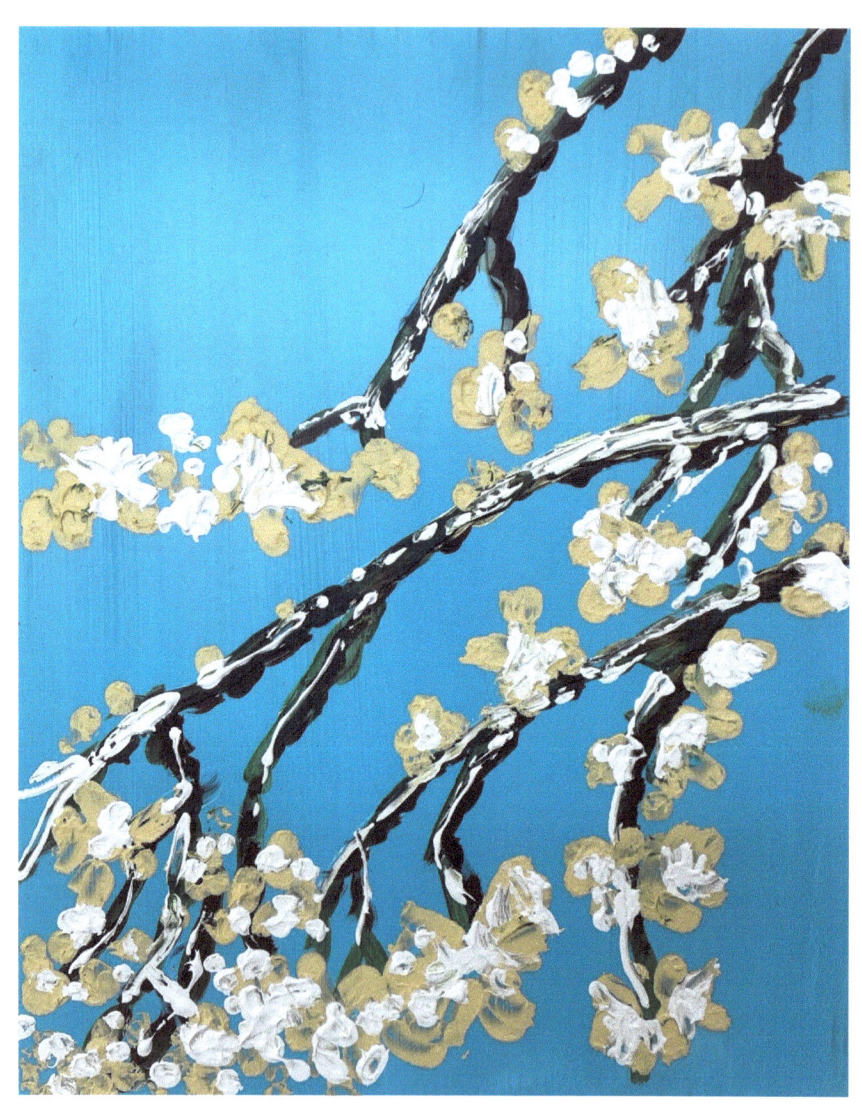

Almond blossom 2
Acrylic on board, 200x240mm

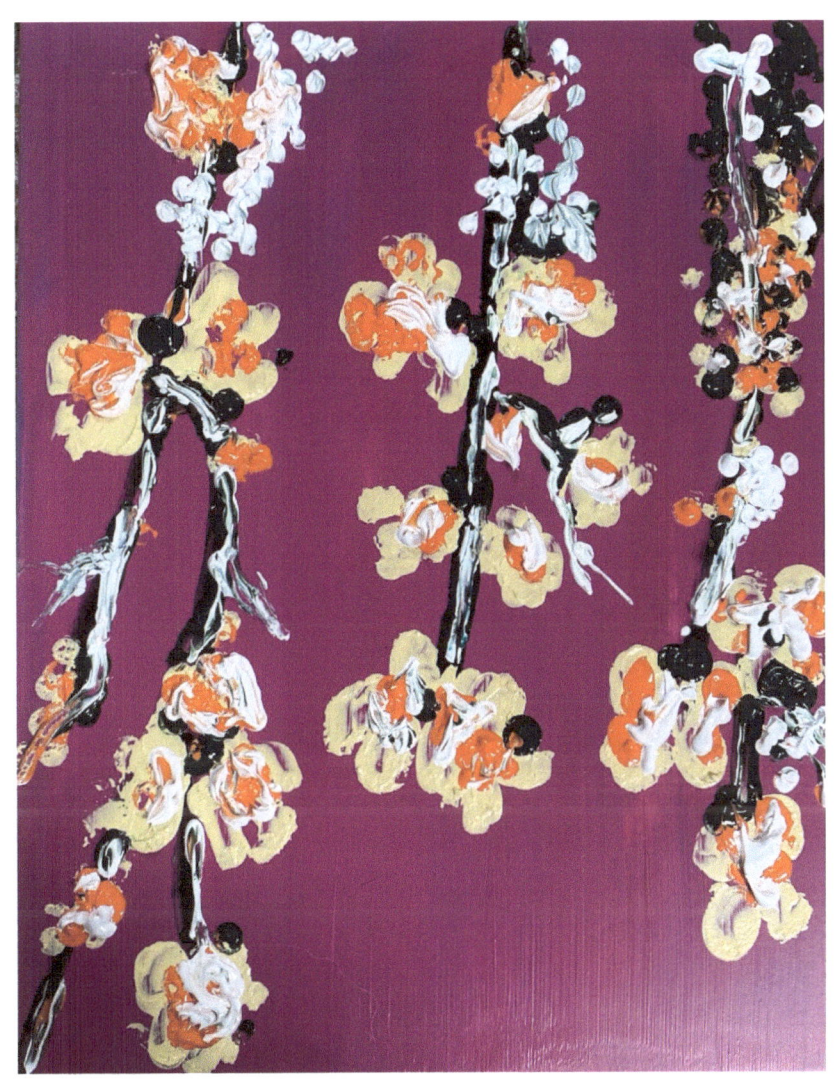

Almond blossom 3
Acrylic on board, 200x240mm

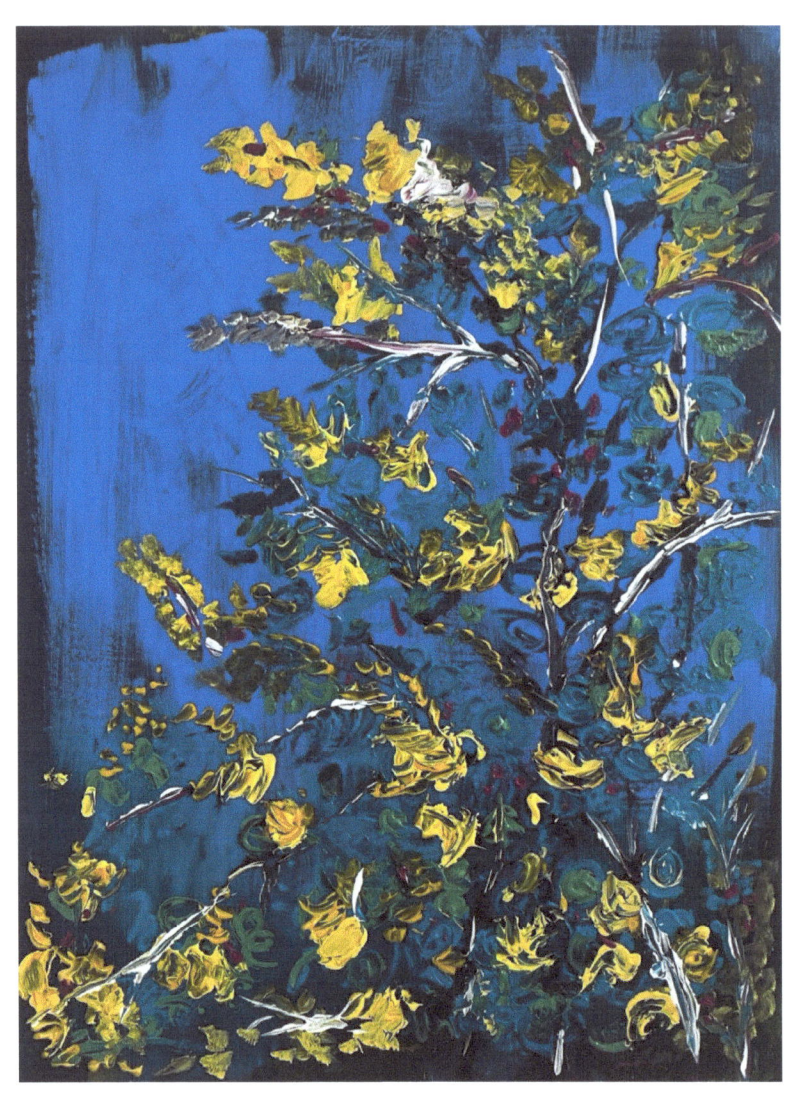

Gorse & Spring wild flowers
Acrylic on canvas, 600x800mm

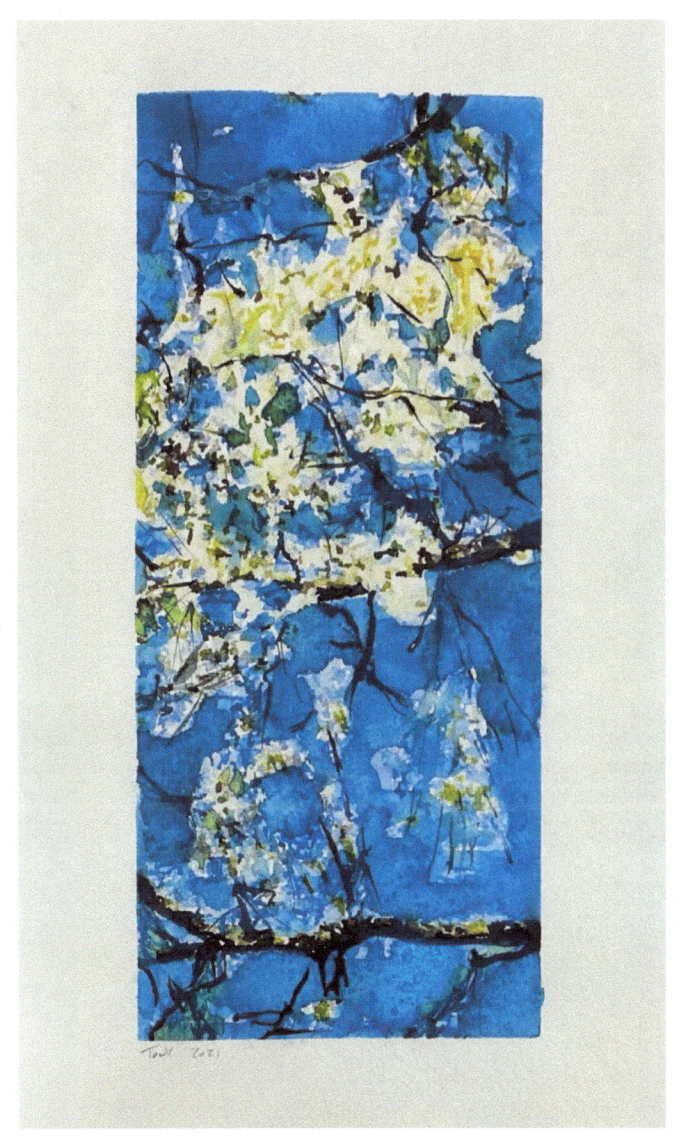

Cherry blossom & blue sky
Watercolour on paper, 300x400mm

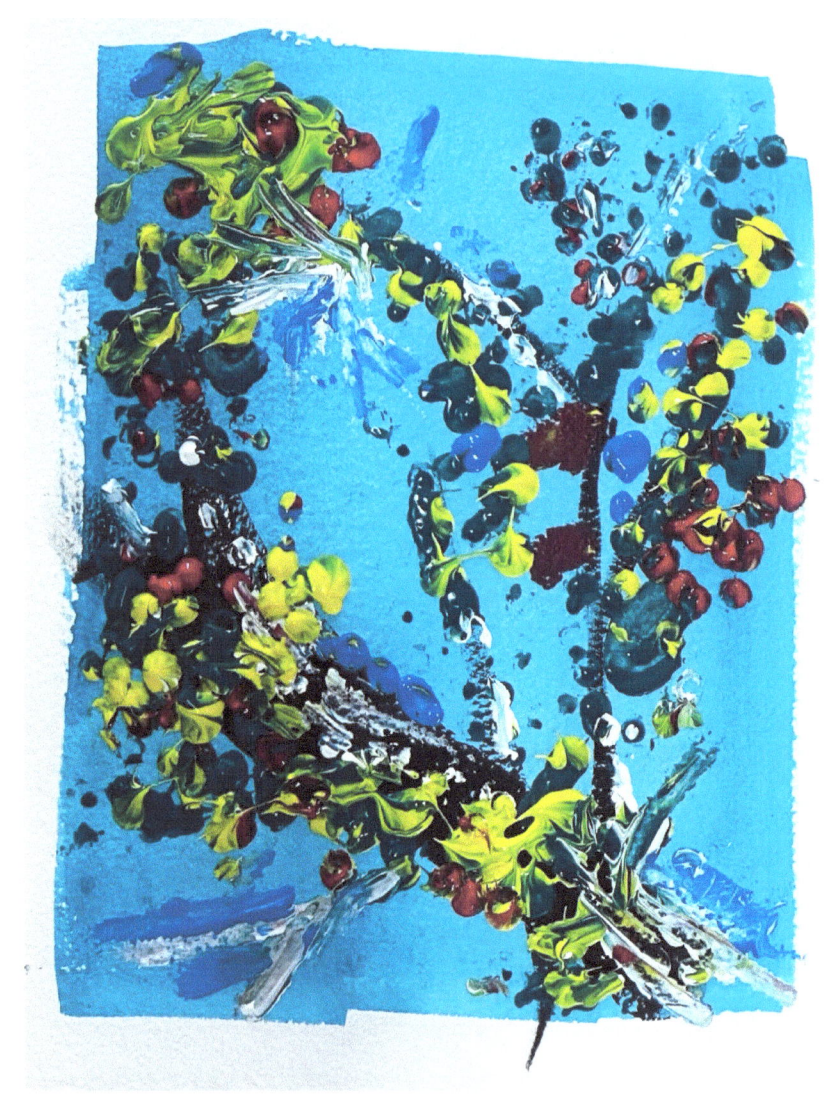

Vibrant Hanami

Watercolour & Guaché in sketchbook, 200x240mm

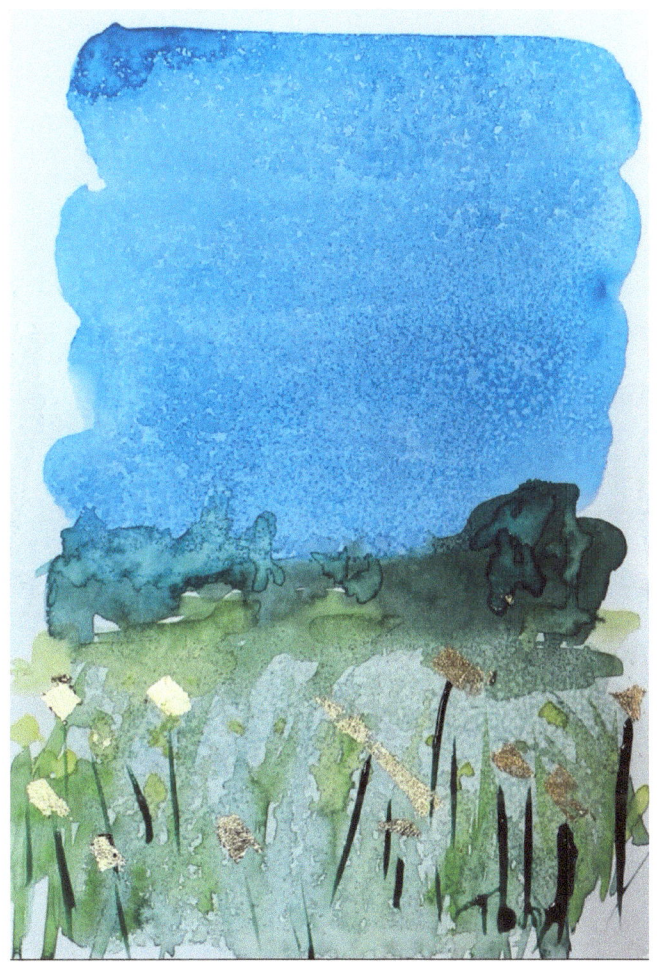

Field flowers with gold
Watercolour & Gold leaf on paper, 140x190mm

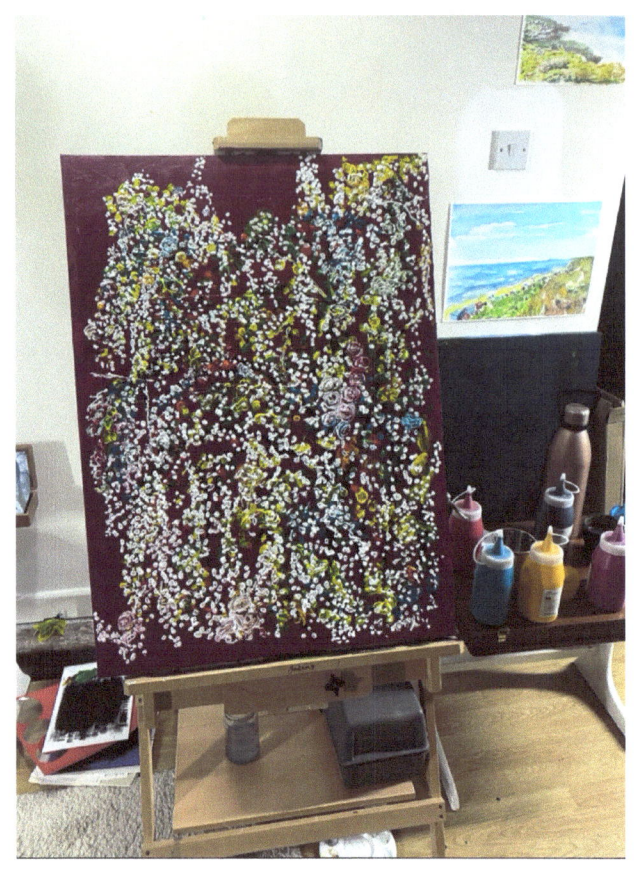

'In progress at the studio'

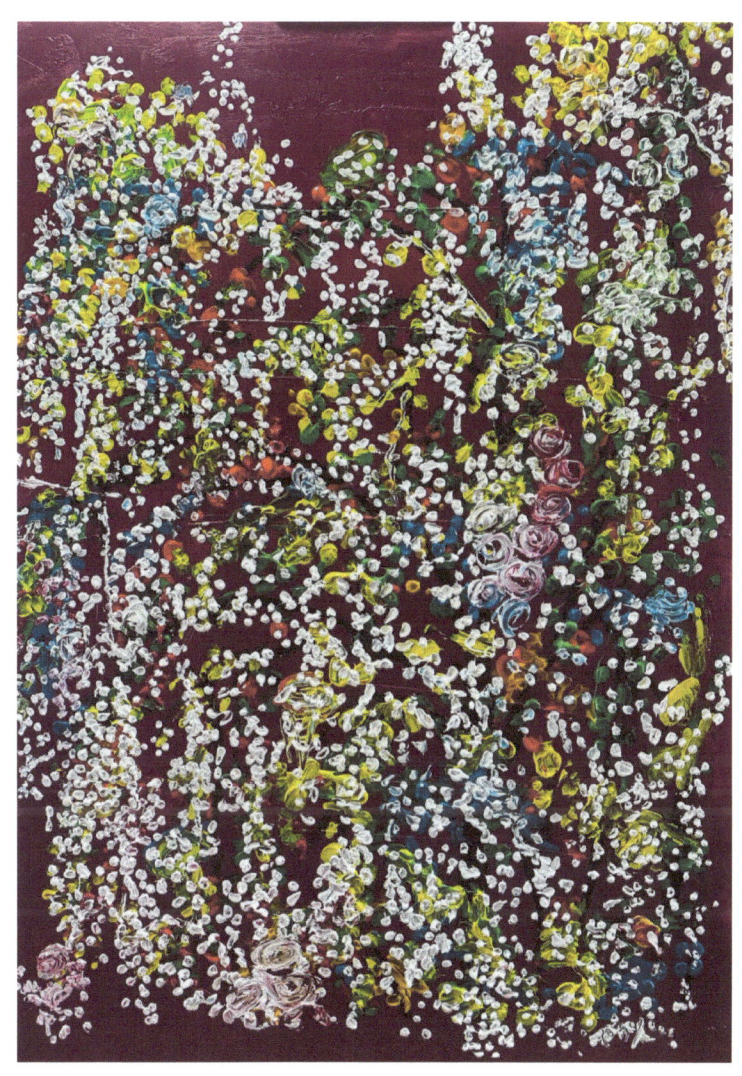

Mandela Meditation on calm
Acrylic on canvas, 600x800mm

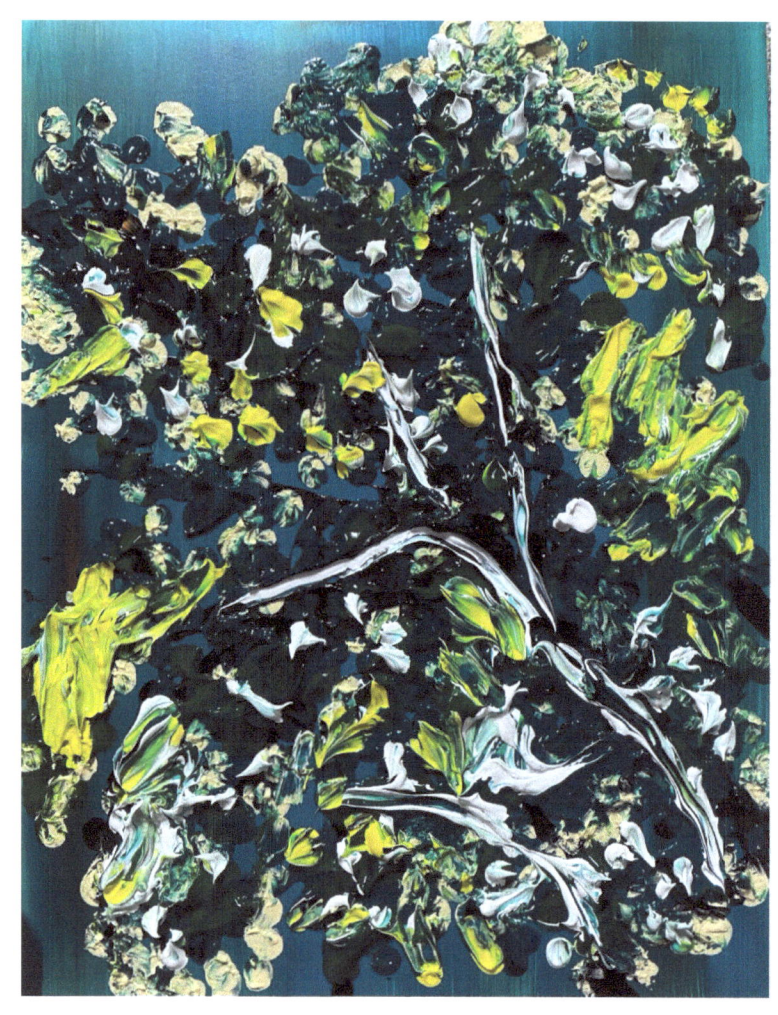

Hedgerow
Acrylic on board, 200x240mm

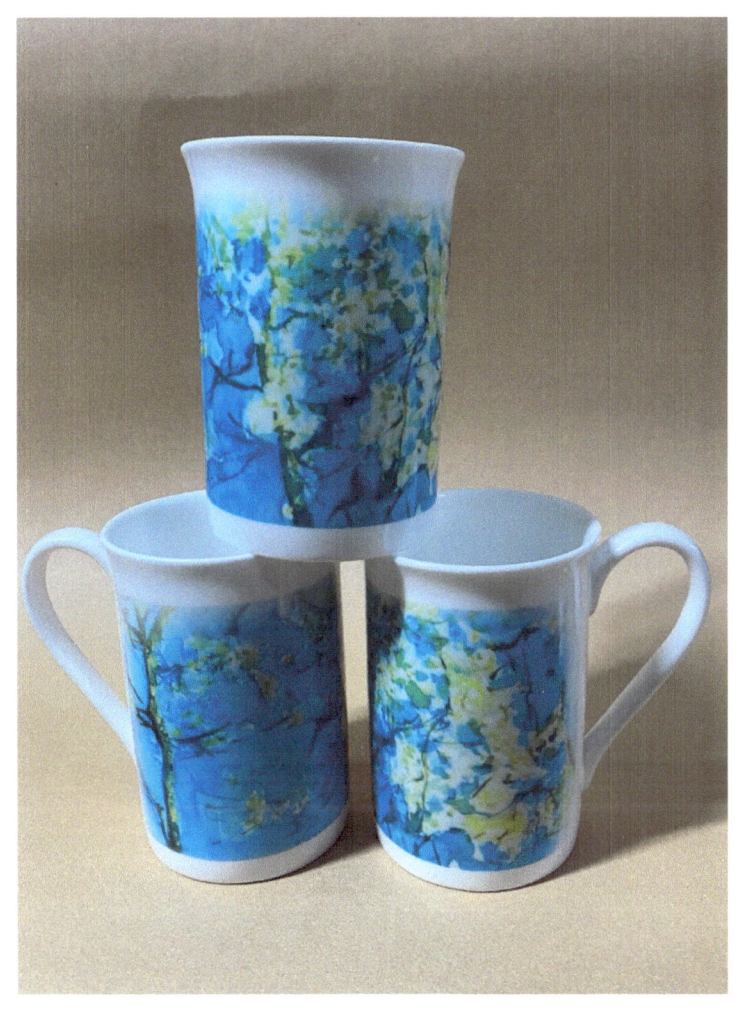

Hanami on chinaware
Hand printed & pressed illustrations on china-ware.

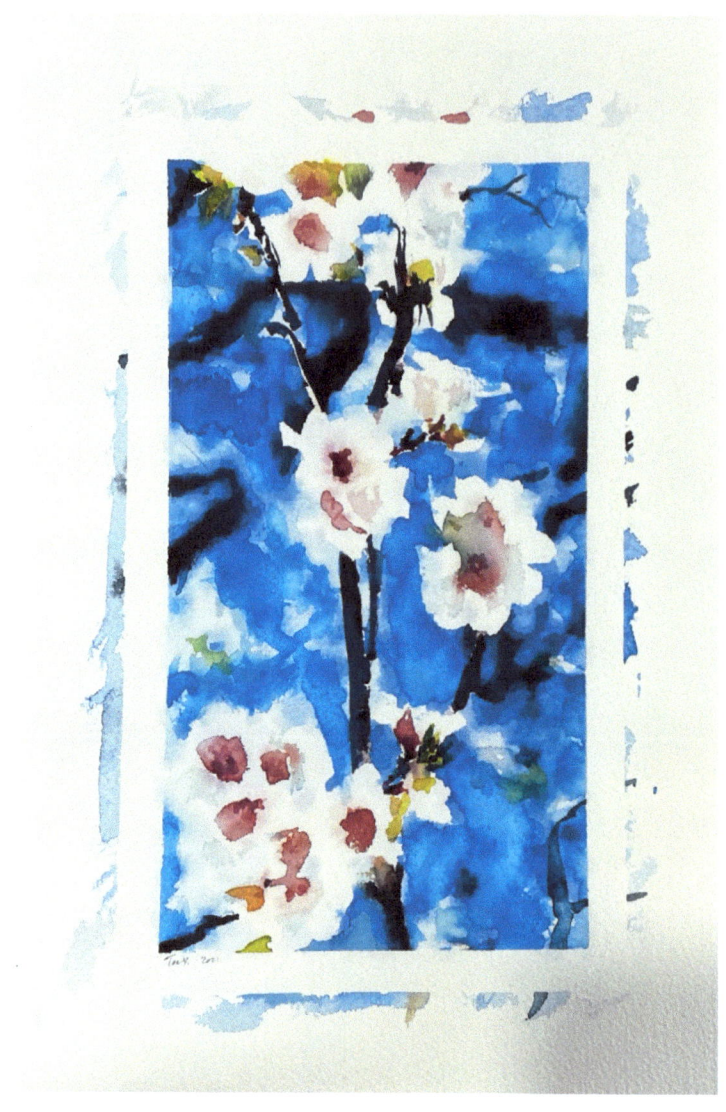

Cherry Blossom & blue
Watercolour on paper, 300x400mm

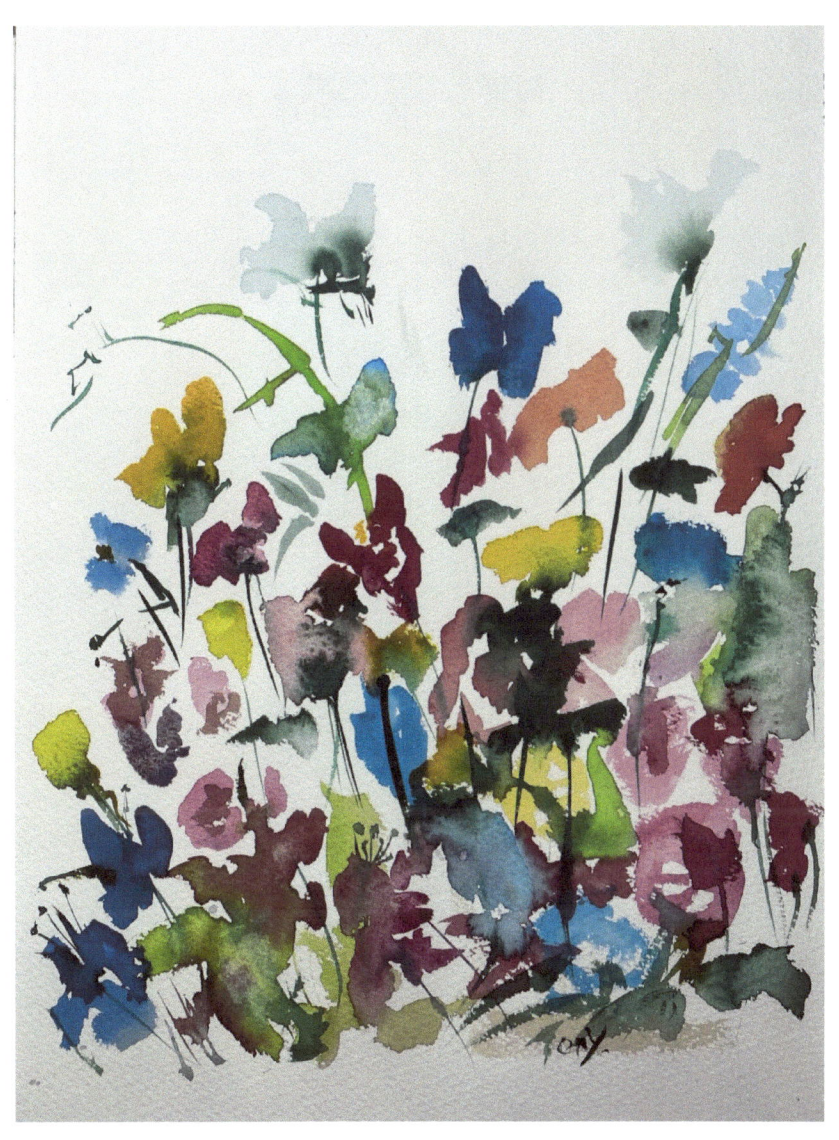

Spring Wild Flowers

Watercolour on paper, 300x400mm

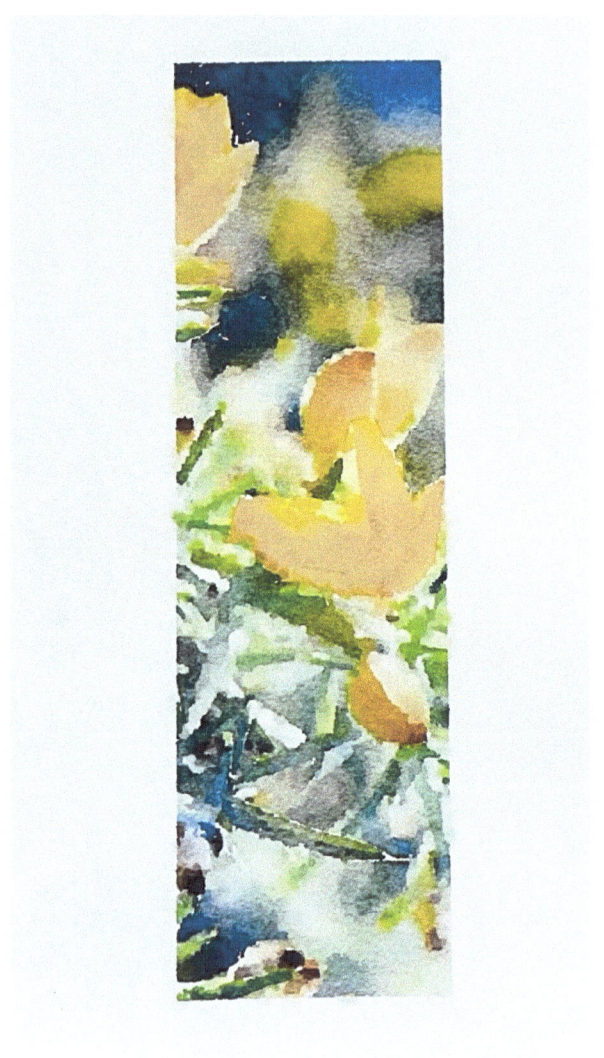

Gorse flowers in frost
Watercolour on paper, 300x400mm

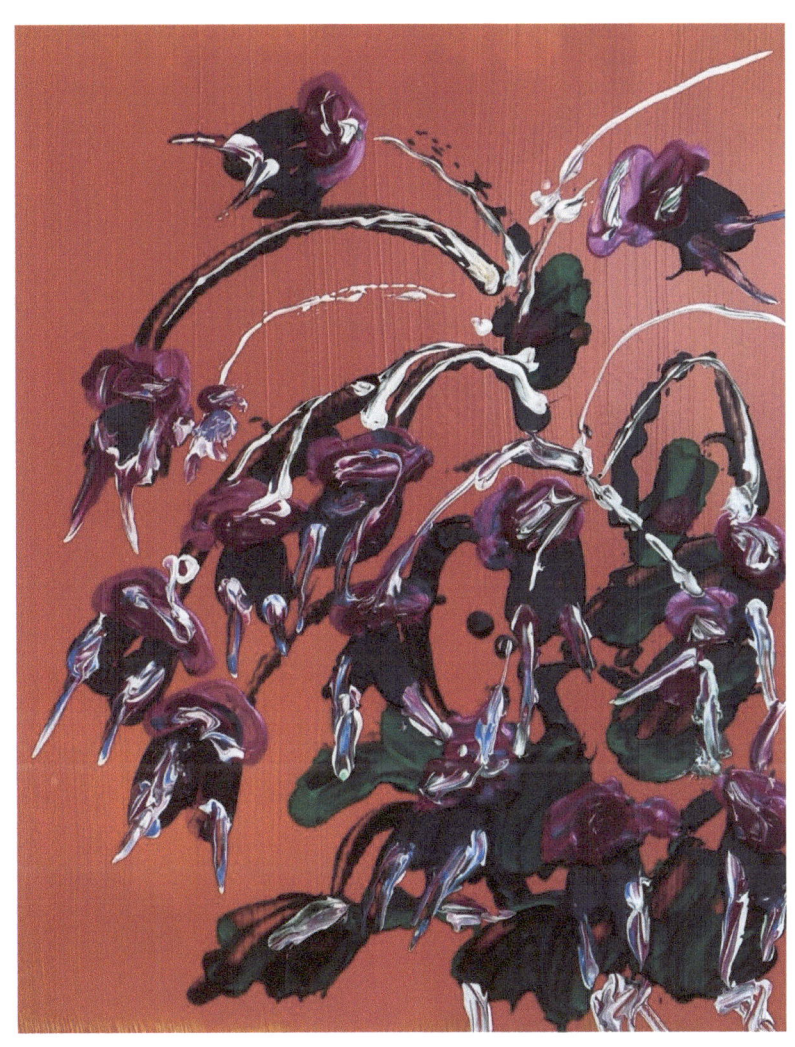

Falling fuscias 2
Acrylic on board, 200x240mm

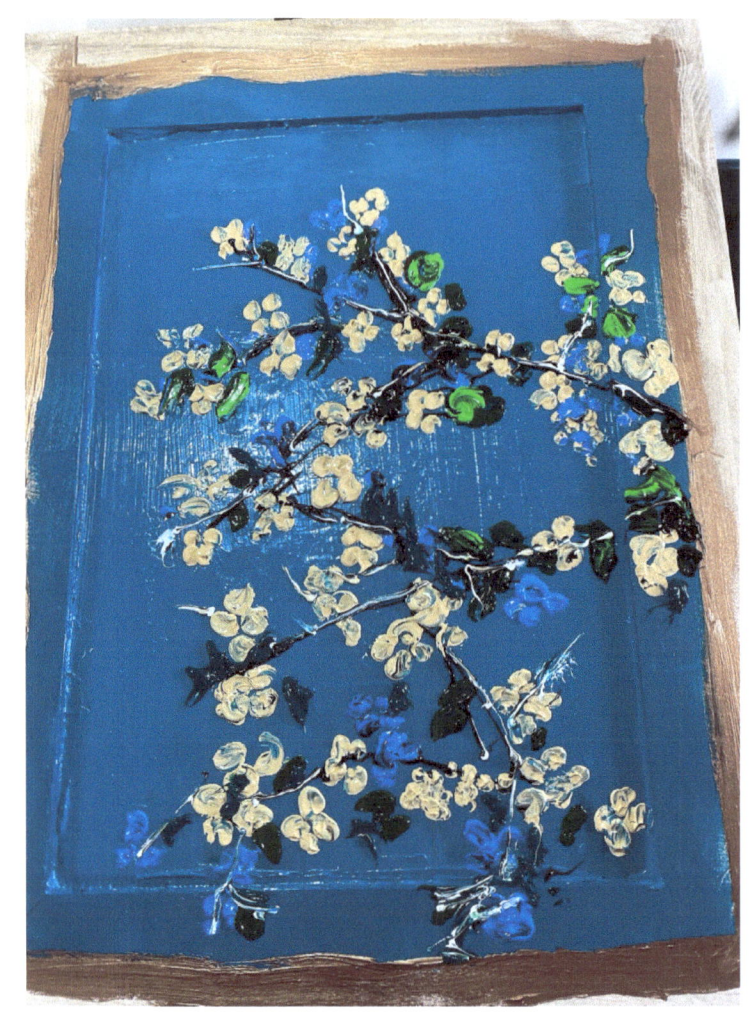

Almond door
Acrylic on recycled door panel, 1000x1300mm

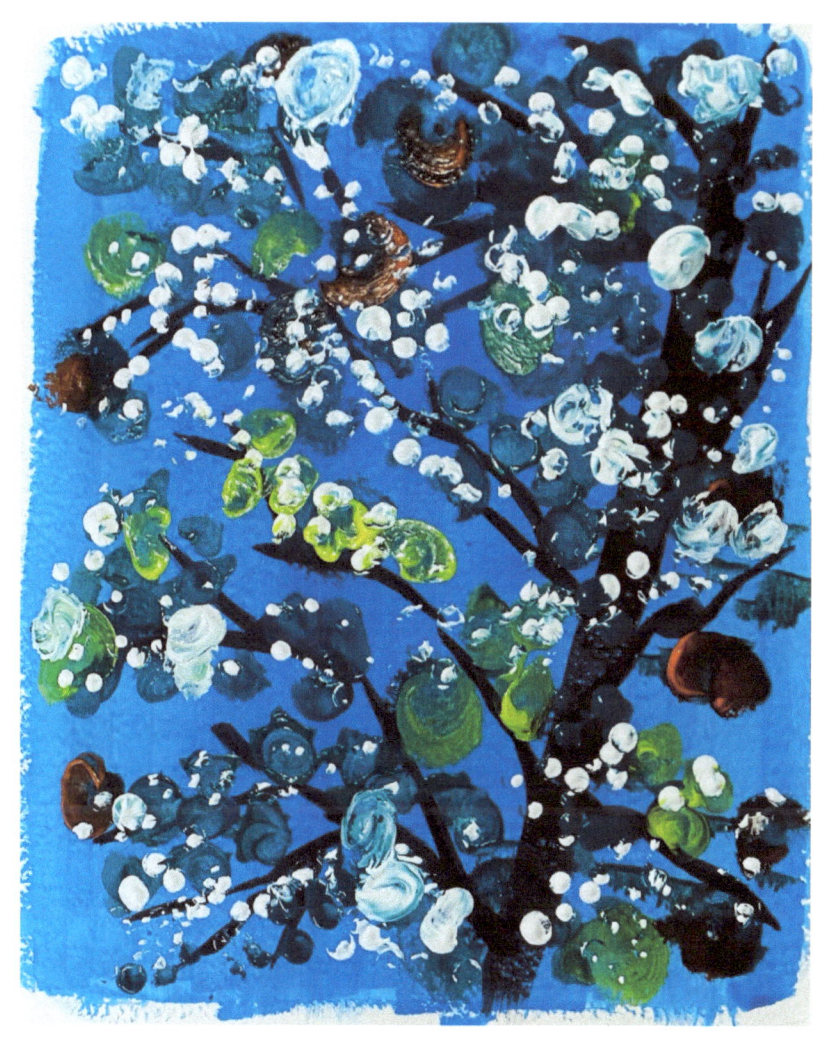

Hanami Sketch
Watercolour in sketchbook, 200x240mm

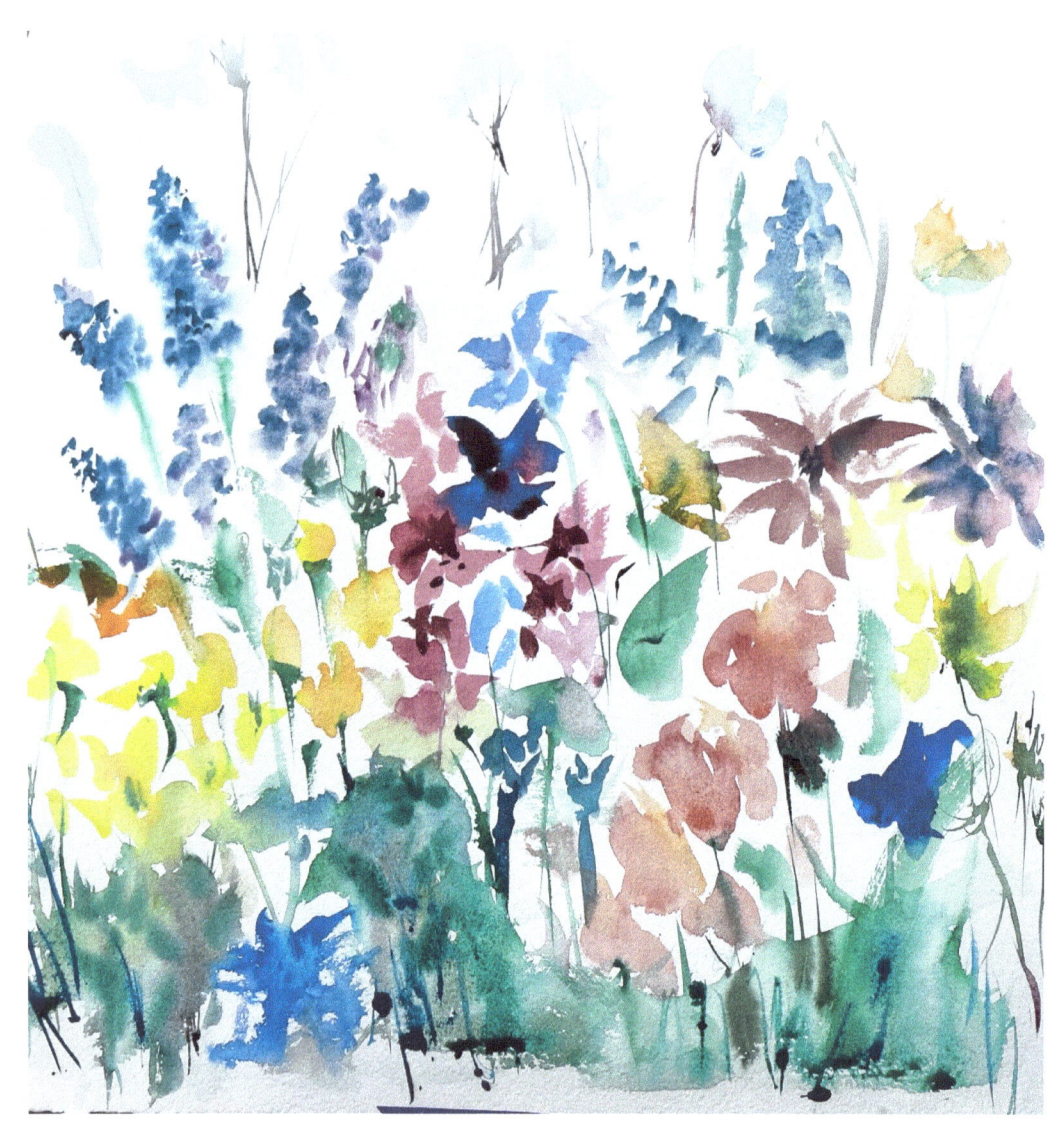

Wild Flowers

Watercolour on rag paper, 500x500mm

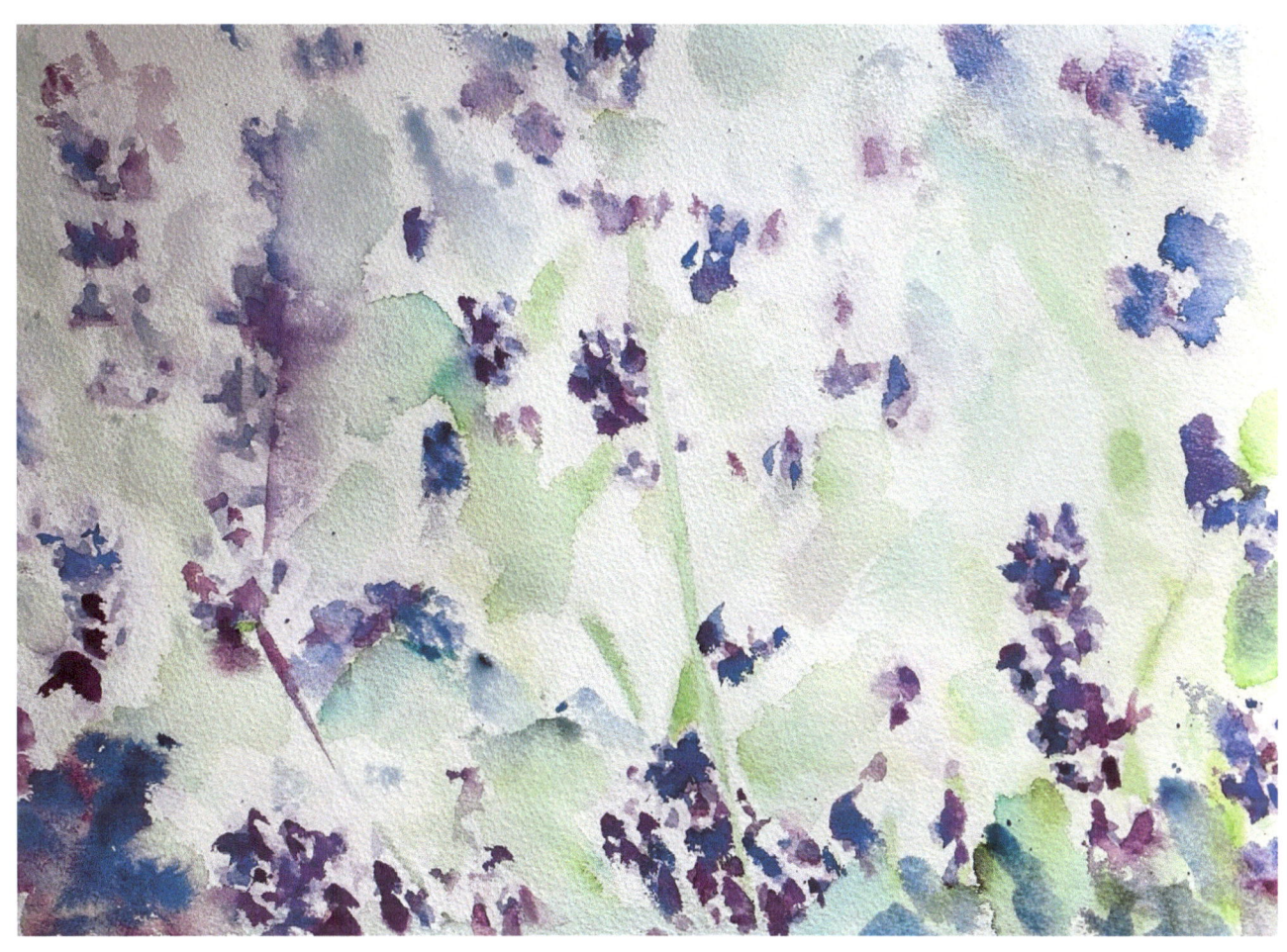

Lavender
Watercolour on paper, 400x300mm

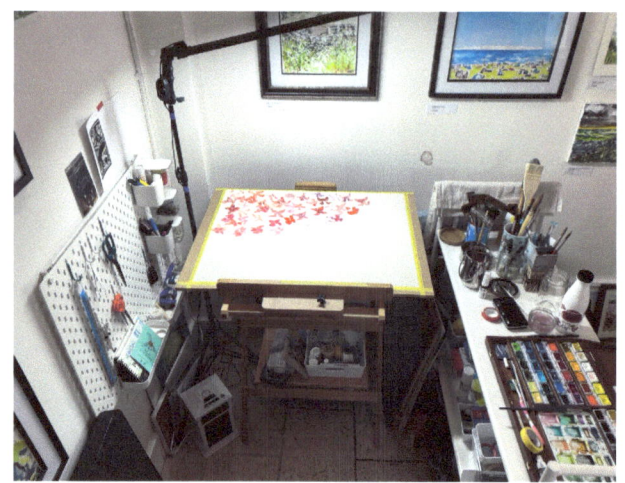
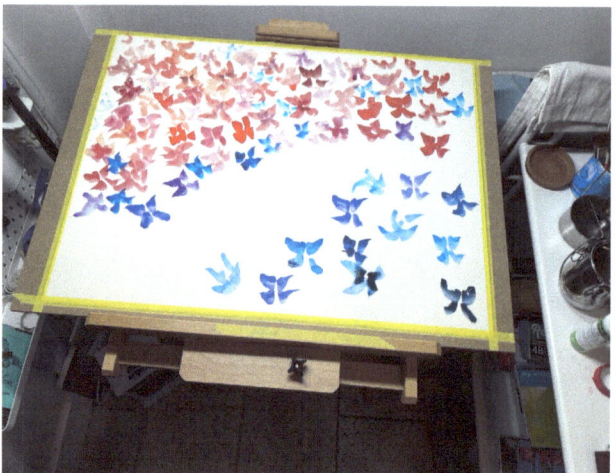

Spring flowers in progress. Painted in my old studio, during the dreary January of 2021.

This large watercolour has gone on to be one of my most successful paintings, and now the foundation of a product range based on my love for furniture and homeware design.

You can see examples of this translation from watercolour to fabric and chinaware over the following pages.

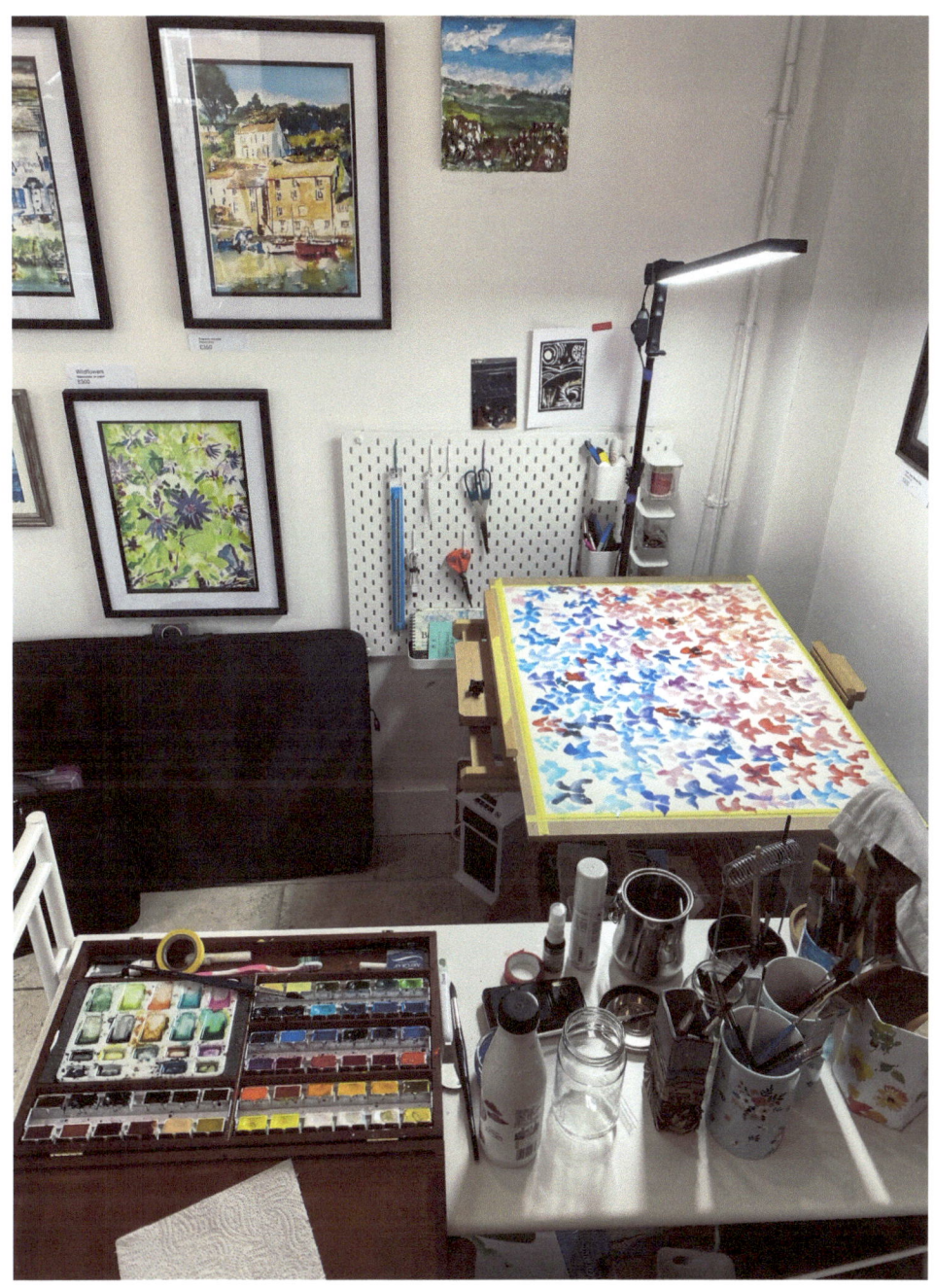

Spring Flowers, 2021
Watercolour on paper, 800x600mm

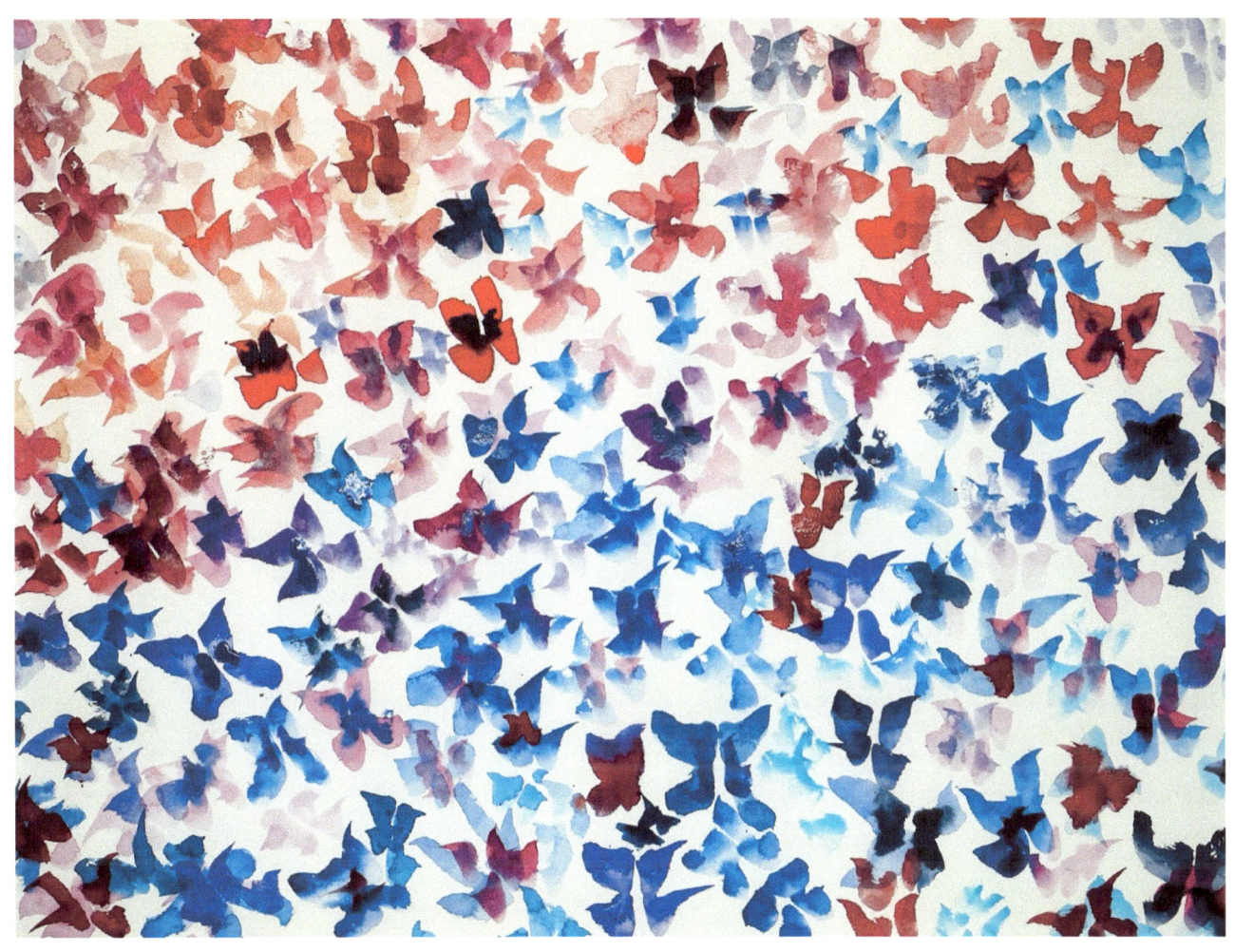

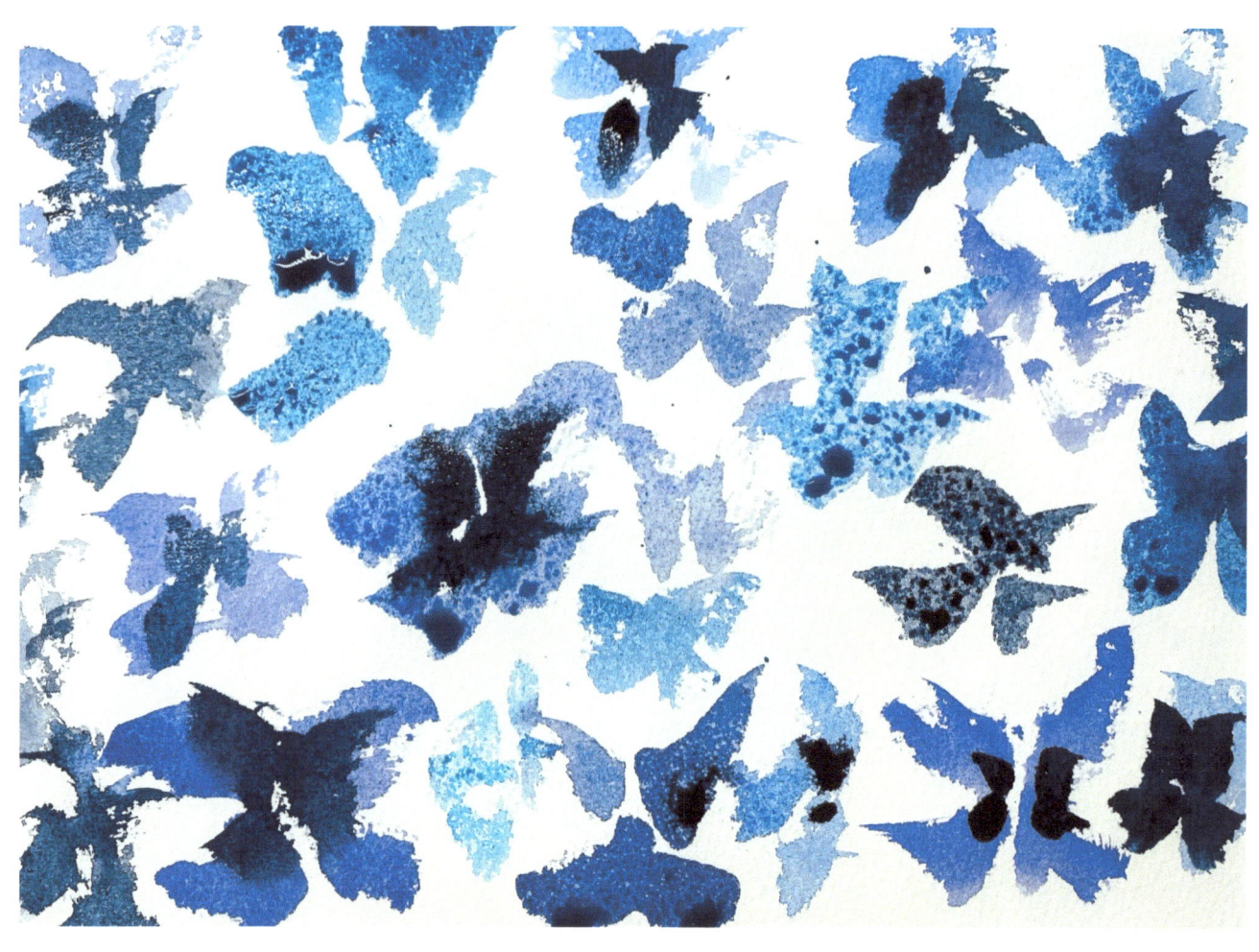

Blues Spring Flowers, 2021
Watercolour on paper, 400x300mm

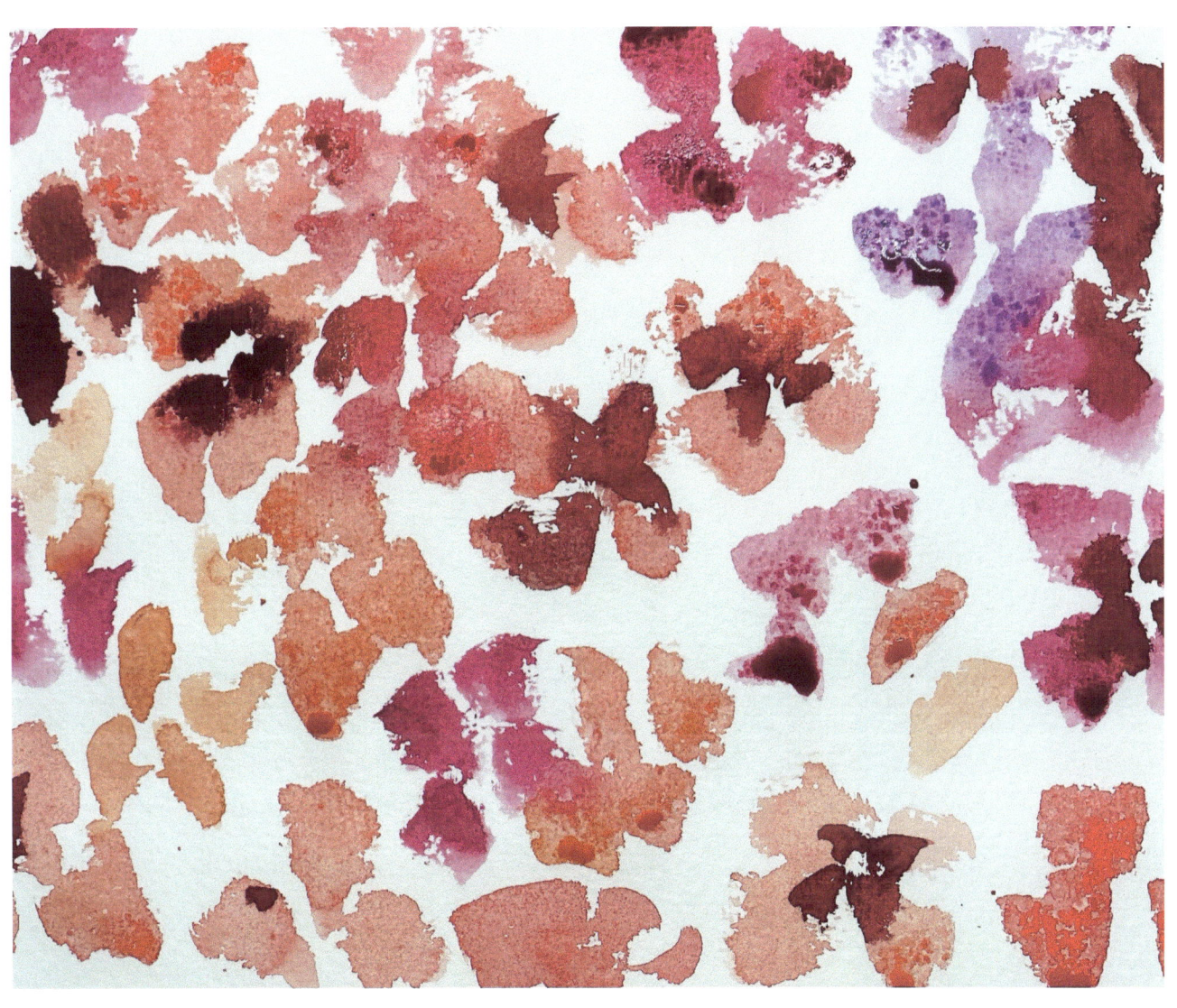

Pinks Spring Flowers, 2021
Watercolour on paper, 400x300mm

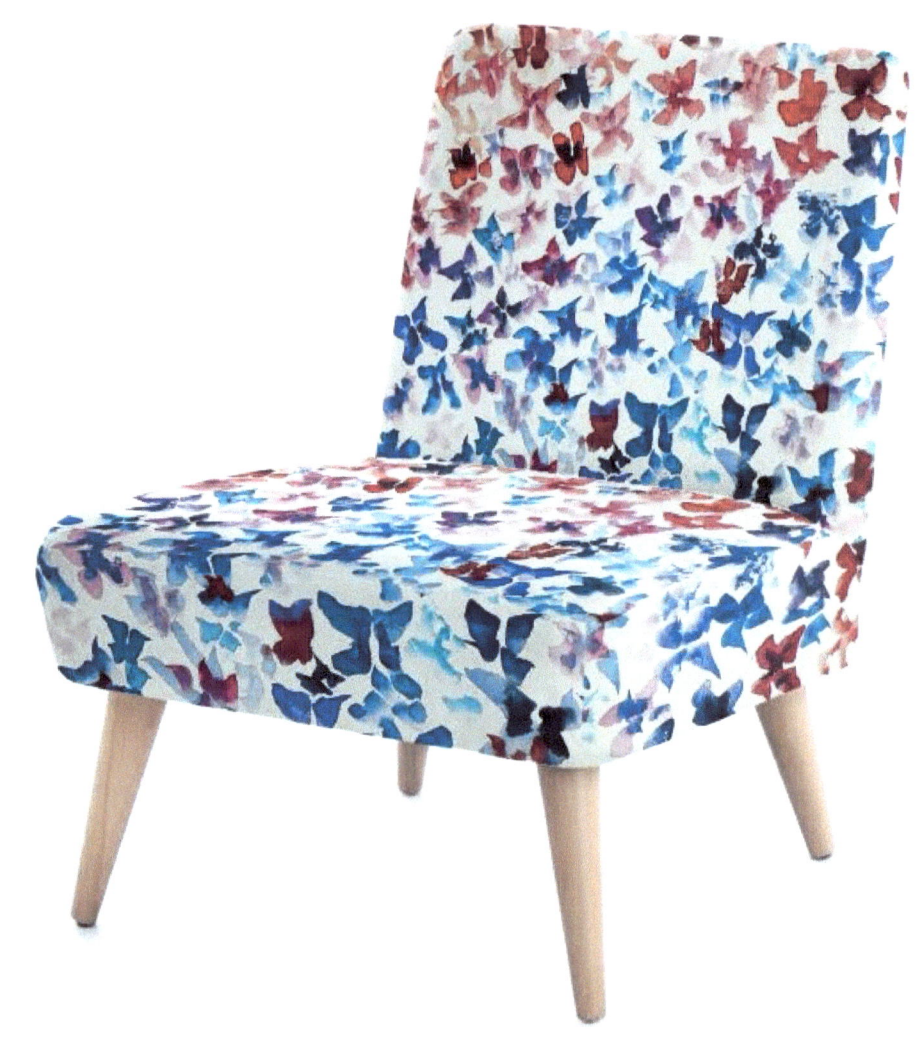

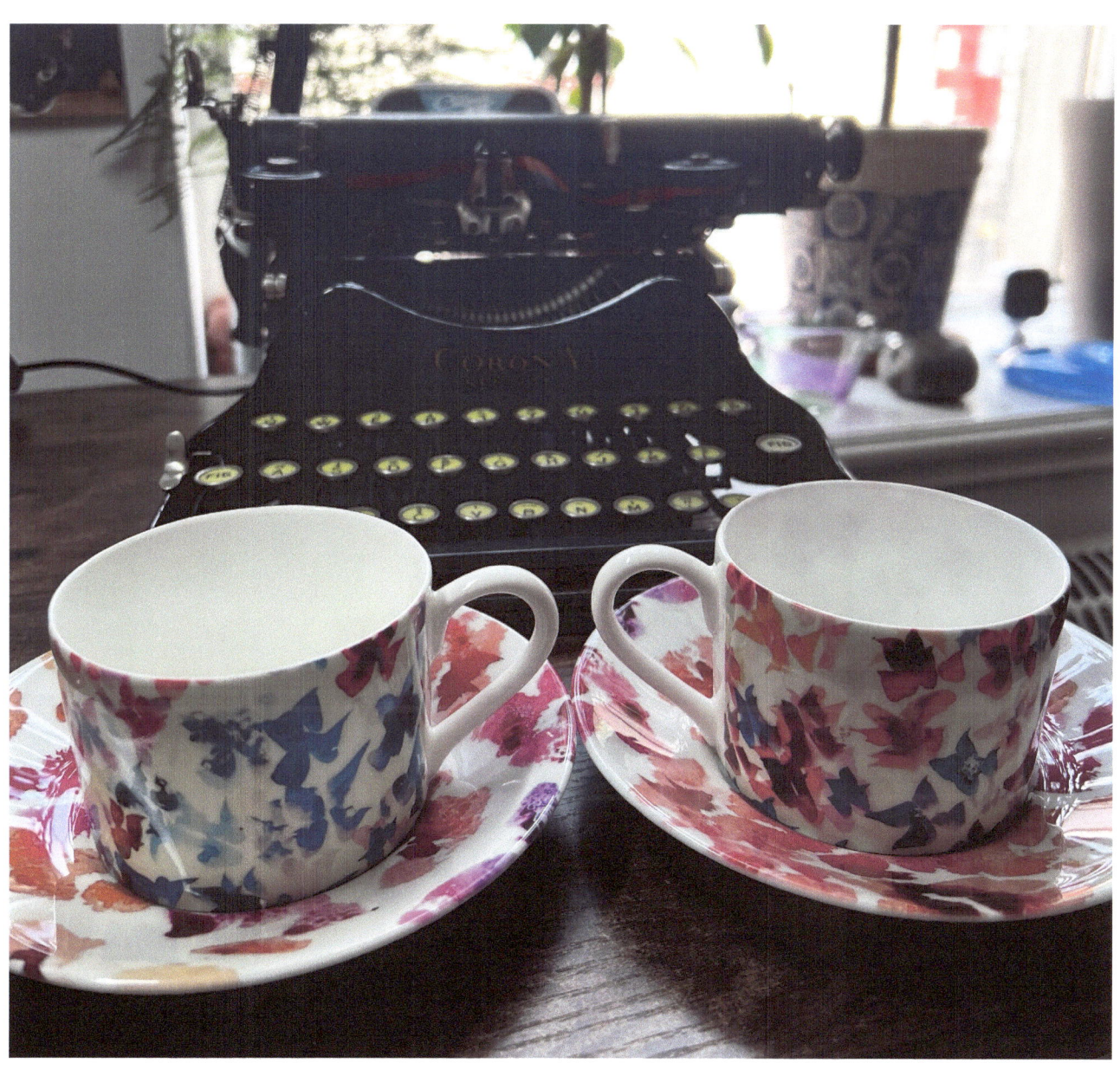

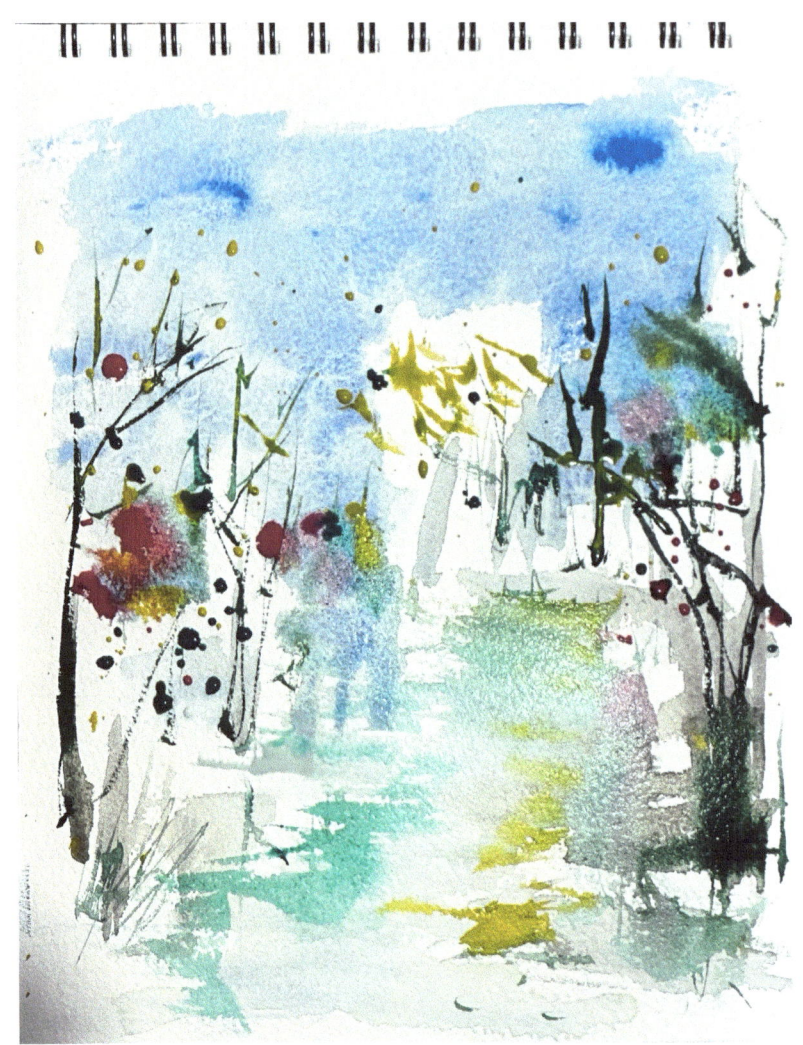

Sketchbook work: Cherry Tree Walk in bloom
Watercolour on paper, 300x210mm

HOPE.
COLOUR.
JOY.

THANK YOU

Tony Malone.

www.ingramcontent.com/pod-product-compliance
Lightning Source LLC
Chambersburg PA
CBHW051216220526
45473CB00003B/1057